Focus on Oral Interaction

Oxford Key Concepts for the Language Classroom series

Focus on Assessment
Eunice Eunhee Jang

Focus on Content-Based Language Teaching
Patsy M. Lightbown

Focus on Oral Interaction
Rhonda Oliver and Jenefer Philp

Focus on Oral Interaction

Rhonda Oliver
Jenefer Philp

OXFORD
UNIVERSITY PRESS

OXFORD
UNIVERSITY PRESS

Great Clarendon Street, Oxford, OX2 6DP,
United Kingdom

Oxford University Press is a department of the University
of Oxford. It furthers the University's objective of excellence
in research, scholarship, and education by publishing
worldwide. Oxford is a registered trade mark of Oxford
University Press in the UK and in certain other countries

ACKNOWLEDGEMENTS

*The authors and publisher are grateful to those who have given permission
to reproduce the following extracts and adaptations of copyright material:*
pp.5, 15, 22, 52 Extracts from 'When the gate opens: the interaction
between social and linguistic goals in child second language
development' by J. Philp & S. A. Duchesne from *Second Language
Acquisition and the Younger Learner: Child's Play?* edited by J. Philp,
R. Oliver & A. Mackey. John Benjamins Publishing Company, 2008.
Reproduced by kind permission of John Benjamins Publishing
Company, Amsterdam/Philadelphia, www.benjamins.com. p.11
Extract from 'Task Familiarity and Interactional Feedback in Child
ESL Classrooms' by A. Mackey, A. Kanganas & R. Oliver, TESOL
Quarterly Vol. 41 Iss. 2, 2007. © TESOL International Association.
Reproduced by permission of John Wiley and Sons, Inc. p.13
Extracts from 'The Patterns of Negotiation for Meaning in Child
Interactions' by R. Oliver, The Modern Language Journal Vol.
86 Iss. 1, 2002. © Blackwell Publishers Ltd 2002. Reproduced by
permission of John Wiley and Sons, Inc. pp.14, 96, 98 Extracts from
*Making Language and Learning Work 2: Integrating language and learning
in Secondary English and Social Sciences* by Ministry of Education,
New Zealand, 2008. Reproduced by permission of Learning Media
Limited. p.17 Extract from 'L1 use in primary and secondary foreign
language classrooms and its contribution to learning' by Rita
Tognini & Rhonda Oliver from *Discourse and language learning across L2
instructional settings.* Utrecht Studies in Language & Communication
Vol. 24, 2012. Reproduced by permission of Editions Rodopi B.V.
pp.21, 28 Extracts from 'Teaching Content, Learning Language:
Socialising ESL Students into Classroom Practices in Australia' by
R. Oliver & J. McLellan in *Creating Classroom Communities of Learning
International Case Studies and Perspectives* edited by R. Barnard &
M. E. Torres-Guzmán. Published by Multilingual Matters, 2009.
Reproduced by permission of Multilingual Matters. pp.30, 38–39,
49, 104, 107, 109–10 Extracts from 'Interaction in languages other
than English classes in Western Australia primary and secondary
schools: Theory, practice and perceptions' by Rita Tognini, 2008.
Reproduced by permission of Rita Tognini. p.44 Extract from
Learning to Learn in a Second Language by Pauline Gibbons, Primary
English Teaching Association Australia (PETAA), Sydney, pp.27–8.
Reproduced with permission from PETAA – Primary English
Teaching Association Australia. p.45 Extract from 'Age Differences
in Negotiation and Feedback in Classroom and Pairwork' by Rhonda
Oliver, Language Learning Vol. 50 Iss. 1, 2000. © Language Learning
Reasearch Club, University of Michigan. Reproduced by permission
of John Wiley and Sons, Inc. pp.46, 71–2, 74 Extracts from *Bridging
Discourses in the ESL Classroom: Students, Teachers and Researchers* by
Pauline Gibbons. Published by Continuum, 2006. © Pauline Gibbons
2006. Reproduced by permission of Bloomsbury Publishing Plc.
p.50 Extract from *Audible Difference ESL and Social Identities in Schools*
by Jennifer Miller. Published by Multilingual Matters Ltd, 2003.
© Jennifer Miller 2003. Reproduced by permission of Multilingual
Matters. p.74 Extract from 'Home–school connections for
international adoptees: Repetition in parent–child interactions'
by Lyn Wright Fogle from *Second Language Acquisition and the Younger
Learner: Child's Play?* edited by J. Philp, R. Oliver & A. Mackey.
John Benjamins Publishing Company, 2008. Reproduced by kind
permission of John Benjamins Publishing Company, Amsterdam/
Philadelphia, www.benjamins.com. p.78 Extracts from 'Language
Learning: The Importance of Access to Community' by Kelleen
Toohey & Elaine Day, TESL Canada Journal Vol. 17 Iss. 1, 1999.
Reproduced by permission of TESL Canada Journal. p.82 Extract
from '"Breaking Them Up, Taking Them Away": ESL Students in
Grade 1' by Kelleen Toohey, TESOL Quarterly Vol. 32 Iss. 1, 1998.
© TESOL International Association. Reproduced by permission of
John Wiley and Sons, Inc. pp.85–86 Extract from 'How Young is
too Young? Investigating Negotiation of Meaning and Feedback in
Children Aged Five to Seven Years' by Rhonda Oliver from *Multiple
Perspectives on Interaction: Second Language Research in Honor of Susan
M. Gass* edited by Alison Mackey and Charlene Polio. Published by
Routledge, 2010. Reproduced by permission of Taylor and Francis
Group LLC Books. pp.87, 92, 106 Extracts from 'Rehearsing,
conversing, working it out: Second language use in peer interaction'
by Rita Tognini, Jenefer Philp and Rhonda Oliver, Australian
Review of Applied Linguistics Vol. 33 Iss. 3, 2010. Reproduced by
permission of Australian Review of Applied Linguistics. pp.100,
101 Extracts from 'Intertextuality and Hybrid Discourses: The
Infusion of Pop Culture in Educational Discourse' by Patricia A
Duff, Linguistics and Education Vol. 14 Iss. 3–4, 2003. Reproduced
by permission of Elsevier Limited. p.102 Extract from 'Teachers'
knowledge and experience in the discourse of foreign-language
classrooms' by Manel Lacorte, Language Teaching Research Vol. 9
Iss. 4, 2005. Reproduced by permission of SAGE Publications. p.105
Extract from 'Language acquisition in foreign language contexts
and the differential benefits of interaction' by Jenefer Philp & Rita
Tognini, International Review of Applied Linguistics in Language
Teaching Vol. 47 Iss. 3–4, 2009. Reproduced by permission of Walter
de Gruyter GmbH. p.111 Extract from 'Interaction and Second
Language Learning: Two Adolescent French Immersion Students
Working Together' by Merrill Swain and Sharon Lapkin, Modern
Language Journal Vol. 82 Iss. 3, 1998. © The Modern Language
Journal. Reproduced by permission of John Wiley and Sons, Inc.
p.112 Extract from 'The effect of interaction in acquiring the
grammar of a second language' by Folkert Kuiken & Ineke Vedder,
International Journal of Educational Research Vol. 37 Iss. 3–4,
2002. Reproduced by permission of Elsevier Limited. pp.113, 114,
115 Extracts from ''Co-constructing'' Explicit L2 Knowledge with
High School Spanish Learners through Guided Induction' by Paul
D. Toth, Elvis Wagner and Kara Moranski, Applied Linguistics Vol.
34 Iss. 3, 2012. Reproduced by permission of Oxford University
Press. pp.118–19 Extract from 'Age-Related Differences in the
Motivation of Learning English as a Foreign Language: Attitudes,
Selves, and Motivated Learning Behavior' by Judit Kormos & Kata
Csizér, Language Learning Vol. 58 Iss. 2, 2008. © Language Learning
Research Club, University of Michigan. Reproduced by permission
of John Wiley and Sons, Inc.

Sources:
Canadian Modern Language Review
British Educational Research Journal

Instructed second language acquisition: Case studies by R. Erlam & K. Sakui

To our wonderful friends and family, especially Martin, Kathryn and Mike; Andrew, Ellie, Myles, and Henry for distracting us, and keeping us grounded.

Contents

Acknowledgments

Firstly, thank you Patsy Lightbown and Nina Spada. We cannot imagine a more incredible editing team. We are truly grateful for your wise counsel, patience, and unflagging encouragement. Your perceptive feedback and indefatigable eye for detail have made all the difference.

Thanks also to the other amazing SLA people who set the scene, and taught us much: Rod Ellis, Sue Gass, Mike Long, and Alison Mackey.

A special thanks to friends and colleagues within the field and especially those who helped with our research and generously shared their own data and insights: Rebecca Adams, Susan Duchesne, Mike Exell, Ellen Grote, Yvonne Haig, Noriko Iwashita, Judith Rochecouste, and Rita Tognini.

Acknowledgments

Series Editors' Preface

The Oxford Key Concepts for the Language Classroom series is designed to provide accessible information about research on topics that are important to second language teachers. Each volume focuses on a particular area of second/foreign-language learning and teaching, covering both background research and classroom-based studies. The emphasis is on how knowing about this research can guide teachers in their instructional planning, pedagogical activities, and assessment of learners' progress.

The idea for the series was inspired by the book *How Languages are Learned*. Many colleagues have told us that they appreciate the way that the book can be used either as part of a university teacher education program or in a professional development course for experienced teachers. They have commented on the value of publications that show teachers and future teachers how knowing about research on language learning and teaching can help them think about their own teaching principles and practices.

This series is oriented to the educational needs and abilities of school-aged children (5–18 years old) with distinct chapters focusing on research that is specific to primary- and secondary-level learners. The volumes are written for second language teachers, whether their students are minority-language speakers learning the majority language or students learning a foreign language in a classroom far from the communities where the language is spoken. Some of the volumes will be useful to 'mainstream' teachers who have second language learners among their students, but have limited training in second/foreign language teaching. Some of the volumes will also be primarily for teachers of English, whereas others will be of interest to teachers of other languages as well.

The series includes volumes on topics that are key for second language teachers of school-age children and each volume is written by authors whose research and teaching experience have focused on learners and teachers in this age group. While much has been written about some of these topics, most publications are either 'how to' methodology texts with no explicit link to research, or academic works that are designed for researchers and postgraduate students who require a thorough scholarly treatment of the research, rather than an overview and interpretation for classroom practice. Instructors in programs for teachers often find that the methodology texts lack the academic background appropriate for a university course and that the scholarly works are too long, too difficult, or not sufficiently classroom-oriented for the needs of teachers and future teachers. The volumes in this series are intended to bridge that gap.

The books are enriched by the inclusion of *Spotlight Studies* that represent important research and *Classroom Snapshots* that provide concrete examples of teaching/learning events in the second language classroom. In addition, through a variety of activities, readers will be able to integrate this information with their own experiences of learning and teaching.

Introduction

In this book we will examine oral interaction theory and research as it pertains to child and adolescent second language learners. We will provide guidance to primary and high school teachers about pedagogical implications based on the findings of oral interaction research undertaken in the classroom as well as 'laboratory' settings. Although much has been written about oral interaction research, the focus has often been on older learners. We hope this book, with its emphasis on children and adolescents in primary and high school contexts, will serve to redress this.

The content of our book has relevance to teachers in several different settings—for example, those who teach migrant children who are learning the language of the classroom and wider community; those who are involved in Content-Based Language Teaching through a second language; and those teaching **foreign language** students (for example, English speaking students in an English speaking country learning Japanese, French, Spanish, etc.).

In Chapter 1, we outline what oral interaction is, and what it is not. We discuss oral interaction in more detail and as with other books in this series, we use Classroom Snapshots to illustrate the content. Key areas covered in Chapter 1 are the differences between speaking and writing, and the reciprocal nature of speaking and listening. A brief description of how oral interaction develops is also provided.

Chapter 2 explores the role of interaction for second language learning from linguistic, cognitive, social, and pedagogical perspectives. We first examine the features of interaction, including the types of communicative strategies that we all use, but especially those that child language learners engage in. We provide descriptions and examples showing how interaction provides second language input for learners, and also opportunities for learners to provide and to modify their own language output. We explore the related concepts of 'negotiation for meaning' and feedback within classroom activities and the research on how they facilitate language development. We also highlight the challenge that many child learners face as they are developing their oral proficiency in the target language while learning both the language and academic content simultaneously. An examination of the social perspectives of classroom interaction includes a focus on the role of scaffolding for learning, and of language development from a sociocultural perspective. In this section, we discuss the connection between social relationships and the differential benefits of teacher–student and peer interaction for learning.

Chapter 3 explores the contribution of interaction between primary school teachers and their students and between peers in the primary school classroom. We look at how this contributes to the second language acquisition process and to the learners' academic, social, and cultural success. We explore what research suggests about the outcomes of different tasks, when used in different contexts, and also other learner and classroom factors. We also examine the role of first language use in second language classrooms. We then highlight the social importance of interaction for children—how it aids learning, enjoyment, and motivation for this age group.

Chapter 4 provides a parallel exploration of the areas highlighted in Chapter 3, but with a focus on high school-aged learners. We examine the particular challenges facing second language learners of this age as they interact for social and academic purposes, and as they develop their oral interaction abilities to do so. We consider the particular challenges faced by adolescents required to perform tasks which require higher levels of cognitive skill and academic knowledge and as they prepare for life beyond school. We explore ways in which older children are able to make use of developing metacognitive abilities for learning and the implications of this for teaching grammar. Finally, we explore the contribution of cognitive factors such as aptitude and memory, as well as personality and affective factors such as attitudes and motivation, on oral interaction. We then consider how these factors might mediate the potential role of interaction in second language learning in the context of school.

In Chapter 5, we return to the ideas first introduced in Chapter 1 and conclude with a summary of issues and concepts covered in the book. We revisit some common perceptions and beliefs concerning oral interaction as a way of consolidating readers' understanding of the key principles arising from the research presented in this book and their implications for teaching.

1

Oral Interaction

Preview

This book is about oral interaction and is designed to inform teachers—current and future—about the roles and features of this aspect of our language use. Of particular interest for teachers is how important oral interaction is for **second language** development, and for learning to use a second language to get information and to understand subject matter content at school.

Oral interaction is an integral part of our human communication. Be it on the phone, face-to-face, or even over the internet with video links, almost all of us will spend some time each day speaking and listening to others. We might chat on the phone to a friend, talk to a cashier at the shops, make a booking at restaurant, or order our lunch at the cafeteria. We interact orally for many reasons: to get things done, to share our feelings, and to make and maintain relationships.

Oral interaction is also integral to learning a language. It is a vital part of pedagogy. In schools, students will talk with and listen to their teachers and they will chat with their peers. Although some teachers may not like their students talking during class time, others will actively plan for students to talk as part of their lessons. They do so recognizing the contribution that oral interaction can make to language and literacy development.

Clearly oral interaction is a key part of what we do as teachers. However, possibly because we all interact so often and because we have a general level of understanding of what oral interaction involves, we rarely stop to reflect on what we really mean when we use this term, especially in an educational context. If we listen to educators or look at curriculum documents, terms such as 'oral interaction', 'communication', or 'speaking' and 'listening' are used frequently and interchangeably, but often without first being clearly defined.

In this chapter we will describe oral interaction, what it is and what it is not, how it differs from written language, and how different aspects of oral interaction contribute to its success or failure as a mode of meaningful communicative exchange. We will illustrate the different concepts we cover by using excerpts from transcripts of actual classroom conversations—written records of oral interactions between various individuals. Many of these are taken from studies we have conducted with students who were learning a second language, but also with mainstream school-aged students—some of whom were interacting with second language learners.

Before we go into these details, we would like you to reflect upon your own perceptions about and attitudes to oral interaction.

Activity 1.1

The statements below represent views that some people hold about oral interaction. Read each statement and check one of the columns to indicate how much you agree or disagree with it. Keep a copy of your responses as we will return to these questions in Chapter 5.

SA = Strongly agree   A = Agree   D = Disagree   SD = Strongly Disagree

		SA	A	D	SD
1	Language learners don't need to be taught how to speak as they pick it up in the classroom. It is more important to focus on reading and writing.				
2	Oral interaction activities are most useful for helping learners practice language they already know.				
3	It is too hard for students to use the target language in the classroom all the time.				
4	It is more useful for students to practice speaking with the teacher in the whole class than with each other in groups.				
5	Speaking the target language with other students in pairs and groups just reinforces mistakes.				
6	Speaking the target language can be fun and motivating, but students learn more by writing and reading, or studying grammar.				
7	Scripted role-play is the most useful speaking practice because students use the target language correctly without mistakes.				
8	Pair-work and group-work interaction between learners is useful because it is motivating and less stressful than whole class interaction.				
9	It is just as important to develop students' social speaking skills as it is to develop their oral language for academic purposes.				
10	Context makes all the difference to how we say things.				

What Is Oral Interaction?

Oral interaction is the spoken language that takes place between two or more people and, as the name implies, it is the type of speaking and listening that occurs in real time (i.e. in the present) in communicative exchanges (i.e. interactions). Usually it entails the speakers talking in turn and responding orally to these turns, though sometimes speakers interrupt or talk 'over' each other. Oral interaction is **collaborative** and most often **reciprocal**, with each speaker working to co-construct a meaningful exchange. For example, the complementary nature of interaction may be as simple as one learner agreeing with the other, as in the case of Classroom Snapshot 1.1 when two older **primary** (elementary) school-aged English as a Second Language (ESL) students chat **off-task**.

Classroom Snapshot 1.1

1 **A:** I'm hungry.
2 **B:** Me too.

(Oliver, Philp, & Duchesne, unpublished data)

The complementary nature of interaction can also be very complex, especially when there are more than two people involved. In Classroom Snapshot 1.2, three kindergarten children talk as they build a long pattern on the floor using flat blocks. One of the three, Yessara, is a new pupil who is learning to use English as an additional language whereas Sam and Roberta are native speakers (NS) of English. As for all data in this book, the names are pseudonyms. Appendix 1 provides a summary of transcription conventions used.

Classroom Snapshot 1.2

1 **Yessara:**   This one this one this one one big one.
2 **Sam:**   Yes the biggest one in the whole wide world.
3 **Yessara:**   Big!
4 **Sam:**   Da da da da da da da.

[later turn]

5 **Yessara:**   Thi:s one. [adding to blocks with Roberta]
6 **Yessara:**   Too long Roberta.
7 **Roberta:**   This is gonna be excellent.
8 **Sam:**   Wonder if we'll be able to use all these blocks.
9   That'd be fun if we could use all these blocks wouldn't it?
10 **Yessara:**   XX lot block … bi:g one block.

(Philp & Duchesne, 2008, p. 94)

A little like their block building, the children's talk reflects the co-constructive nature of oral interaction—what one person says depends on, and adds to, what was said before. Philp & Duchesne suggest that Yessara's interaction with her peers in this activity provided her with both a **model** of language (note the complexity of Sam's language in line 9), and a context for using language. Further, interacting with her peers helps her become a part of this classroom community. In Chapter 2, we will see that interaction serves both linguistic (learning language and learning to use language) and social (being part of a community) functions.

While oral interaction can occur at a distance, such as over the phone, it is mostly done face-to-face and because of this we can see how our conversational partners react and so responses can be non-verbal. That is, while we describe such talk as oral interaction, not all responses need to be spoken. Exchanges may include gestures and physical responses such as nods, shrugs, pointing, or even **paralinguistic** responses such as clicks or whistles. The key aspect of oral interaction is that it is *interactive*. For instance, Classroom Snapshot 1.3 is part of an interaction between an adult (R), a non-Aboriginal teenager (M), and an Australian Aboriginal teenager (G), whose English language proficiency is quite limited as he mainly speaks a traditional Indigenous language.

Classroom Snapshot 1.3

1 **M:** What are you doing?
2 **G:** [points to his head]
3 **R:** Did you get hurt?
4 **G:** [nods head and clicks tongue]

(Oliver, unpublished data) ▪

Although G does not speak out loud, he is very much part of the exchange and is just as involved in the oral interaction as M or R.

In summary, oral interaction is collaborative in that it is co-constructed by two or more participants and most often reciprocal in nature. It consists of speaking and listening as well as non-verbal and paralinguistic features. Generally, it is very different from written language and it is this difference that we turn to next.

Comparing Speaking and Writing
Differences

Consider Texts 1 and 2 below. They were elicited as part of classroom research with learners of a similar age (middle primary school) who have been learning English as a second language for a similar period of time (approximately six months). Reflect upon which is the oral interaction text and which is the written text.

Text 1

1 My first sister was born in a Karen state. Her name is Cherry Win. She was born in hospital.
2 My second sister was born in a Karen state. Her name is Herry Say. She was born in a Karen state, too. She likes to cook and sing.

Text 2

1	**Teacher:**	Where do you live?
2	**E:**	… Ah, in Australia.
3	**Teacher:**	In Australia!
4	**E:**	Mm …
5	**Teacher:**	Oh where do you live?
6	**J:**	Mm Yemen.
7	**Teacher:**	You come from Yemen but where do you live here?

(Oliver, unpublished data)

Although both texts are about similar topics—namely about the background of students—it is not too difficult to determine that Text 1 is a piece of written text whilst Text 2 is an oral interaction. How do we know this? Firstly, the turn-taking and reciprocal nature of Text 2 suggests oral interaction, whereas Text 1 seems like writing, specifically a child's writing. Text 1 also appears more formal and decontextualised (it can be read and understood in a different place at a different time). In Text 2, although we can understand what is going on, we can see that in the exchange the teacher uses repetition and clarification when J does not answer appropriately, and it is through this that J's meaning is made more transparent. In contrast, in Text 1 the text must stand alone and provide sufficient information in a logical and coherent way so readers can understand it all—they do not have the opportunity to ask for clarification from the writer. Also note that although it is quite a simple piece of writing, the vocabulary that is used in Text 1 (for example, 'first', 'second', 'hospital', 'state') is more complex than that which occurs in Text 2. Text 1 consists entirely of complete sentences, but notice that in Text 2, there is **ellipsis**: 'in Australia' means 'I live in Australia.' It is unnecessary to include the whole sentence because the first part is understood from the previous person's utterance.

Similarities

The texts above serve to highlight the important differences between oral interaction and writing (Barton, 1994). Even so there are a number of similarities: both written and spoken texts require the production of language. They are also both constructed for reception: written language is constructed for the reader, spoken language for the listener. They can both serve a wide variety of purposes, for example, sharing background information, inviting a friend to dinner, expressing a difference of opinion, or organizing to get something done. In modern society, being able to communicate well is essential—both through oral interaction and through literate practices.

Typical Linguistic Features

Although what can be achieved through written texts and oral interaction may be similar, the form of the language differs. Oral language usually involves more questions ('What do you mean?'), imperatives ('Sit down'), exclamations ('Stop!'), **deictic** language ('Let's go there') and ellipsis ('In Australia'). In contrast, writing is generally more complex and more complete in structure and will have fewer questions, imperatives, exclamations, and **deixis**, but more passive verb forms. This is particularly true of academic writing, and less true of informal writing (for example, that written in notes or when texting or used for social networking).

Differences in Planning

One of the key points of difference between writing and oral interaction is the planned and unplanned nature of the two. Writing can be thought about, planned, and revised. However, as much as we'd like to, we do not ordinarily plan and cannot really revise what is produced in oral interaction. (How many times would we have loved to erase what we just said out loud!) Oral interaction is spontaneous and ephemeral: unless it is recorded, once spoken it disappears into the ether. On the other hand, there is much more conscious control over written language and it is far more permanent. Because of the planning and control that can be exerted over writing, it can be edited until it is correct. Oral interaction is less than perfect—it consists of **disfluencies**, false starts, unnecessary repetition, and redundant information. Despite this, teachers will sometimes judge oral interaction according to the characteristics of written language. They will correct students' disfluencies in their spoken language, even though these are a natural part of oral interaction and not a sign of an incompetent speaker.

Oral Interaction Instruction

Whilst a great deal of time is spent in mainstream classrooms helping students learn to read and to write, less time is spent teaching students to interact orally. In fact, we would argue that in a child's first language (L1) little, if any, explicit instruction is given about oral interaction at least within the classroom (though some time may be spent on teaching students to 'give a talk'). In a second language classroom, such as an ESL class in New Zealand, or a foreign language classroom, such as a French class in Australia, more emphasis is given to the 'how to' of oral interaction, but generally even second language teachers tend to teach through oral interaction—rather talking about it or teaching students how to do it.

One notable exception to this relates to the **pragmatics** and the appropriacy of the language being used. As native speakers we usually understand what is the right or appropriate thing to say, but because of cultural and linguistic differences these rules of social propriety often need to be taught to second language learners, even when they reach fairly advanced levels. Thus, teachers will work to make explicit and transparent the rules of discourse in the new language, just as they make explicit their expectations about classroom behavior, as seen in Classroom Snapshot 1.4 from a primary school reception class for recently arrived immigrant children who are using English as a second language. After Kevin presents his news of the day, the teacher trains the students in how to respond appropriately.

Classroom Snapshot 1.4

1	**Kevin:**	Thank you for listening to my news.
2	**Teacher:**	Thank you.
3		Well … he just said thank you for listening to his news.
4	**Students:**	You're welcome Kevin.
5	**Teacher:**	Oh wha= you know when you are saying 'You are welcome' who do you look at? Do you look at the person at the person over there? Well let's say it nicely now and look at Kevin.
6	**Students:**	You're welcome Kevin.

7 **Teacher:**   Good now I was very interested in Kevin's news. When Kevin gives his news= or whoever is saying his news you should look at the person. Alright.

(Mackey, Oliver, & Leeman, unpublished data) ■

Oral Interaction Instruction and Literacy Development

Another difference between first and second language learners is in relation to the timing of learning to write. When we learn our first language we first develop speaking and listening—how to interact orally—and we learn to write later. Many second language learners, especially those who learn their new language in school, will learn to interact orally and to read and write in their new language concurrently or, at the very least, with a much shorter time delay between the skills. Some second language learners actually use reading and writing to support the development of their speaking and listening, although this will vary according to the individual characteristics of the learner (see Chapter 4). The reverse is also true—oral proficiency is important to literacy development. For example, in a report based on a review and synthesis of research on literacy development among language-minority students in K-12, in the USA, August & Shanahan (2006) had this to say:

> Instruction in the key components of reading is necessary—but not sufficient—for teaching language-minority students to read and write proficiently in English. Oral proficiency in English is critical as well—but student performance suggests that it is often overlooked in instruction.
>
> (August & Shanahan, 2006, p. 4)

They reported that for these students, successful literacy development, particularly in reading comprehension and writing skills, was related to strong oral proficiency. For this reason, they emphasized the need for extensive oral English development alongside literacy instruction. This is something we will return to in Chapters 3 and 4.

Negotiated Interaction

In the past, writing and speaking were described as 'active' and reading and listening as 'passive' skills, but today this dichotomy is no longer seen to hold true. Just as reading is quite an active process (**decoding** written representation and **encoding** meaning), so too is listening. In oral interaction the participants in a conversation work to share and build understanding, and in all but the rarest conversation this requires active participation.

This is especially the case when native speakers and learners or two learners, such as Anna and Bella in Classroom Snapshot 1.5, are interacting and trying to communicate.

Classroom Snapshot 1.5

1 **Anna:** Where do I put the girl balancing?
2 **Bella:** What? Balancing? What's that?
3 **Anna:** You know … standing on one leg and you not fall down but still standing up so balancing.
4 **Bella:** Oh! Like here standing on one leg on a horse … like this here on the horse.
5 **Anna:** Yeah that's where I going now put it.

(Mackey, Kanganas, & Oliver, 2007, p. 286) ▨

You can see how Bella listens actively and, in response to her lack of understanding, asks questions to clarify the meaning of the word 'balancing'. In second language acquisition research this process is called **negotiation for meaning** or 'negotiated interaction' and it entails the use of communication strategies that enable mutual understanding to be achieved (see Chapter 2). A number of researchers claim that discourse such as this facilitates language learning—in fact, the **interaction hypothesis** developed by Mike Long (1996) is based on this premise. Both child and adult second language learners engage in negotiated interaction, although some age differences exist. These differences, along with other interaction factors that affect language development, are described in Chapters 2 and 3.

Activity 1.2

Look at the following example, which continues the conversation shown earlier in Classroom Snapshot 1.2. The three children continue to build with flat blocks while a parent helper observes. In line 7, the parent responds to the child's utterance with a question, clarifying what Yessara means. In what ways do you think such negotiation for meaning might be useful for the language learner?

1 **Parent helper:** That is such a long long long lo:ng one isn't it Yessara.
2 **Yessara:** Oo eh [you want] make this no.
3 **Parent helper:** Oh you are going to make that one?
4 **Sam:** Mm.
5 **Parent helper:** Are you going to count them all do you think?
6 **Yessara:** No too lots!
7 **Parent helper:** Too many?
8 **Yessara:** Yes too many.

(Philp, unpublished data)

By asking the question 'too many?' the parent helper is able both to clarify the meaning of the language learner's statement, but at the same time model the correct lexical item to be used in this circumstance.

Oral Interaction in Education

Because of its importance to our everyday lives and to students' success socially, academically, and vocationally, in many countries oral interaction is reflected in the curriculum of schools. Sadly, however, as we noted above, oral interaction skills are not usually given the same priority nor described in the same amount of detail as those relating to the development of reading and writing. Many times the skills required for developing oral interaction are implied, rather than explicitly detailed or only some narrow aspects of speaking are included (for example, 'reporting the news') whilst other aspects (for example, disagreeing, expressing sympathy, or offering an alternative opinion) are ignored. It is not surprising, therefore, that many teachers struggle with how best to develop their students' oral interaction skills. It is perhaps for this reason that teachers are not as familiar, nor as comfortable, with teaching oral interaction as they are with teaching reading or writing.

Skills to Learn

Perhaps because of this lack of familiarity or uncertainty about what is required for developing oral interaction skills, some teachers will focus on what Barnes (1976) described as **presentational talk** rather than what he labeled as **exploratory talk**. From our observations in many classes, teachers appear to think that having their students 'give a talk' or do a presentation (such as with PowerPoint) fulfills the speaking component of the curriculum. Although clearly involving spoken language, such 'talks' are only one small part of oral interaction—they are monologues—it is not until the question and answer time (i.e. the time that usually occurs at the end of such exercises when other class members get to ask questions of the speaker) that interaction actually occurs. This is not to say that such presentational language does not have a place in developing a learner's oral language, but rather that it is just one of many aspects to help move learners along the **interlanguage continuum** (i.e. their personal second language developmental journey).

When we use the term 'oral interaction', especially in relation to education and to language learning in particular, we are referring to the many types of communication that occur in classrooms: when teachers and students are discussing aspects of a lesson; when students are jointly working on tasks or activities; when they are engaging in social chit chat, or even when they talk off-task to someone else. Outside of the classroom, oral interaction is the type of talk that occurs between teammates on the sporting field, chat between friends who are out socially together, or between customers and service providers in shopping malls. It is communication that is reciprocal (or complementary), and collaborative in that it is jointly constructed, although it is not always easy! We see an example of this in Classroom Snapshot 1.6, an exchange that occurred between two ESL children. They are working to complete a drawing task: My Phoung is describing a black outline of a simple picture that only she can see (because a barrier has been placed between them) for Frederique to draw.

Classroom Snapshot 1.6

1 **My Phoung:**   It's a= one tree. One tree.
2 **Frederique:**   What?
3 **My Phoung:**   One tree.
4 **Frederique:**   One tree?
5 **My Phoung:**   Yeah.
6 **Frederique:**   One tree.
7 **My Phoung:**   In the=
8 **Frederique:**   =What one t[h]ree mean?
9 **My Phoung:**   Tree.
10 **Frederique:**   One tree!
11 **My Phoung:**   Yes tree. Tree.

(Oliver, 2002, p. 98) ■

Reciprocal Nature of Oral Interaction

The complementary nature of oral interaction is shown as the children work to understand each other and specifically to make clear and to comprehend what is required—namely that Frederique needs to draw a tree (not number three and only one tree, not three trees). Turns are taken and even though understanding is not always achieved immediately, the overall meaning is **scaffolded** until understanding is attained and Frederique goes on to draw the single tree. By engaging in this oral interaction the two learners are able to complete one part of the task they have been set and so the exchange is both interactive and purposeful.

A similar joint construction of meaning occurs as part of the task based oral interaction shown in Classroom Snapshot 1.7. It occurs between a child ESL learner (in this transcript, labeled L) and his native-English-speaking partner (E):

Classroom Snapshot 1.7

1 **L:** Shape like diamond.
2 **E:** Like diamonds?
3 **L:** Yeah. Shape like diamonds.

(Oliver, 1995b, p. 17) ■

Classroom Snapshot 1.8 provides an example of a more academic task carried out by two students in a high school Economics class in New Zealand. The lesson is about Balance of Payments. For this task they must reach consensus on which of three arguments they agree with concerning the Deficit on the Current Account. Jae and Brian, both students with English as an additional language, negotiate content and language as Jae enables Brian to understand his view.

Classroom Snapshot 1.8

1 **Jae:**   It's like sacrificing dead money ... first and then they get when they get profit> you know revenue> and then get profit out of   it> and then they keep on you know repaying the debt=
2 **Brian:** [looking at worksheet, trying to understand] =So debt keep= so the economy keep on paying paying their money bad debt not pay the debt.
3 **Jae:**   No I was talking about the firm.
4 **Brian:** [looking at worksheet] The firm?
5 **Jae:**   Yeah.
6 **Brian:** But the deficit Current Account for the whole economy not the firm?
7 **Jae:**   Yeah I was referring to the firm if the firm cannot operate like that the whole economy cannot operate like that then in the same way kind of idea.
8 **Brian:** [turns to look at Jae, smiling] Oh you're right.

(From DVD, Ministry of Education, New Zealand, 2008) ■

In Classroom Snapshots 1.6, 1.7, and 1.8, the learners are interacting for a very functional purpose—namely to achieve task completion, but interaction can serve other purposes. In Classroom Snapshot 1.9, three school friends are engaged in filling out a lunch order before school. Philp & Duchesne (2010) note that oral interaction such as this can achieve a social as much as a functional purpose. Here, the children's interaction is used to affirm their friendship, as they copy one another's language (as well as one another's lunch orders!).

Classroom Snapshot 1.9

 1 **S:** I'm lunch ordering.
 2 **R:** So am I.
 3 **B:** Is Yessara?
 4 **R:** I dunno ask her.
 5 **B:** Yessara are you lunch ordering?
 6 **Y:** Yes.
 7 **B:** Oh all three of us are! [delighted]
 8 **Y:** Yessara my name is. [writing out lunch order]
 9 **R:** Roberta my name is [copying] too and chicken nugget.
10 **Y:** Chicken=
11 **B:** =Two chicken nuggets.

(Philp & Duchesne, 2008, p. 96) ■

At the same time, it should also be noted that although we are describing oral interaction as being reciprocal, it may not necessarily always be positive. There are many things we can do with oral interaction that can be negative or even critical. For example, as customers we can complain to a service provider, we may argue with our spouse, or on the tennis or basketball court we can dispute a call by the umpire or referee. Teachers are all too aware that students often interact in less than positive ways with each other, such as in Classroom Snapshot 1.10, an interaction between two ESL learners, Charles and Mark, who are completing a task.

Classroom Snapshot 1.10

1 **Charles:**   Put no put a big cross.
2 **Mark:**   Hey you cross too big XX.
3 **Charles:**   No that to do like that before.
4 **Mark:**   No.
5 **Charles:**   Come on.

(Oliver, Philp, & Duchesne, unpublished data) ■

Oral Interactions between Speakers of Different Status

Many of our examples show peers, especially children, interacting with each other. At a general level when peers interact, their status or 'power relationship' is mostly quite even. But of course oral interaction can also occur between speakers of different status. For instance, in a study about 'How Teenagers Talk' (Oliver, Haig, & Rochecouste, 2005) we asked some teenagers how they talk to policemen—their answer 'very, very politely' clearly reflecting their recognition of the difference in power relations. Another situation many of us are familiar with is the interaction in the classroom between a teacher and students. Those of us who have been teachers will know that this does not guarantee that the one with the most power (i.e. the teacher) will necessary control the discourse! Because it is interactive, classroom talk can be just as convoluted as talk between peers. Also, just because it is between a teacher and students does not necessarily mean that the oral interaction is more formal; the discourse can vary greatly just as it does between student peers.

The oral interaction that occurs between a teacher and students can, in fact, be quite informal, such as in Classroom Snapshot 1.11 in a junior primary ESL classroom.

Classroom Snapshot 1.11

1	**Student:**	Frank said he ride the bike with Yan and and he fall in and then he fall in the bum.
2	**Teacher:**	Oh he fell down. Oh dear.
3	**Student:**	And I fall on the botty.

(Oliver & Mackey, 2003, p. 524) ■

The oral interaction between a teacher and students can also be quite formal such as in Classroom Snapshot 1.12, where the high school teacher of Italian is working to make mealtime language meaningful to her students.

Classroom Snapshot 1.12

1	**Teacher:**	*Di solito, a che ora mangi la cena?* [When do you usually have dinner?]
2	**Student:**	*Le 9.30.* [9.30.]
3	**Teacher:**	*La cena la sera. La cena. Non la prima colazione non il pranzo. La cena la sera.* [Dinner in the evening. Dinner. Not breakfast not lunch. Dinner in the evening.]
4	**Student:**	*Alle sei.* [At six.]
5	**Teacher:**	*E di solito cosa mangi come antipasto?* [And what do you usually have for the first course?]

6 **Student:**   *Uumm.*
7 **Teacher:**   *Come antipasto, mangi la bruschetta?* [Do you have 'bruschetta' as first course?]
8 **Student:**   *Uumm mangio la bruschetta.* [I eat bruschetta.]

(Tognini & Oliver, 2012, pp. 66–7)

Scaffolding

Even though more formal, at least in the pedagogical sense, we can also see in the example above that the teacher and student work together in reciprocal ways, with the teacher **scaffolding** the learner's language, shifting from an open question to one that offers the student a possible answer, helping to make their oral interaction meaningful.

Activity 1.3

The following transcripts are taken from two lessons in a primary class for children newly immigrated to Australia, aged 6–7 years.

- What do you notice about the nature of the interaction in these lessons?
- What are some similarities and differences?

Lesson 1: Listening to news and asking questions

In this part of the lesson Kim, a young child, is selected to read out his personal narrative to the class. He reads it without hesitations, without help from the teacher, and without interruptions from his classmates.

The teacher then elicits questions from the rest of the class.

1 **Teacher:**   Right off you go.
2 **Kim:**   On Tuesday I went to play basketball with my Dad and I run with my Dad when I came home and I go to shopping buy me a little toy and I go to my friend to play to the chart? And I got five chips.
3 **Teacher:**   Very good. Give him a clap. Such a good boy Kim. Kim. At the beginning when he came he didn't know hardly any English at all. Now he knows how to write all that very good English. Are there any questions about his news? Alright. Sarah will I get a question from you?
4 **Student:**   Why you go to shopping.
5 **Kim:**   Because my Dad said to go and to to play the chart.
6 **Teacher:**   Good now one question. Is there a question?
7 **Student:**   Why you have fitness in your house?
8 **Kim:**   Because so I can be strong feet and strong hands.
9 **Teacher:**   So he can have a strong body.

Lesson 2: Talking about a shared reading ('Little Red Riding Hood')

In this phase of the lesson, the teacher reviews a story the students have been reading together. He chooses one child, Sunny (S), to do this.

1 **Teacher:**   Select a picture or select a part of the story that you like> Sh [quietens other children] OK now what was the story. Show the picture. Now, what was the stor= what was that part of the story?

2 **Student:**   XX apple pie on the wolf.

3 **Teacher:**   Right [OK] hit the wolf with what?

4 **Student:**   Apple pie.

5 **Teacher:**   With an apple pie. With a plate and had an apple pie on it. Right where did the wolf go from there? When he hit the wolf= when Red riding hit the wolf with an apple pie where did the wolf go to?

6 **Student:**   Went to skateboard.

7 **Teacher:**   Went to where the skateboard was and then what happened to the wolf?

8 **Student:**   The wolf er out.

9 **Teacher:**   Out of the window. Is that right? OK. Give her a clap. And sit down.

(Mackey, Oliver, & Leeman, unpublished data)

Reflection

How does Sunny's interaction differ from Kim's telling of his news? Why?

How does the teacher help Sunny to recount the story?

The teacher responds with repetitions and extensions of Sunny's utterances, as well as questions. Find examples of these in the second lesson—how do these provide scaffolding for Sunny's story?

In these two lessons, we see a difference between what is expected of each child's interaction with others. In each case, a child is called upon to present information to the class. When Kim presents his news, he is able to read from what he has pre-prepared in writing. His speech is quite fluent, he uses complete sentences, and his speech continues uninterrupted until the end. In contrast, Sunny's description of the part of the story he liked best is unplanned. He develops it over many turns, aided by the teacher in different ways. The teacher's turns provide a kind of scaffolding that assists Sunny to tell his story: First the teacher provides a visual aid to remind Sunny of the content and structure the story (line 3). He asks questions that help Sunny to be more coherent and accurate (lines 4–6). Notice how the story is told across turns—Sunny makes a start, the teacher provides a structure and Sunny completes the end '[she] hit the wolf with an apple pie'. He also extends Sunny's utterances (line 7). The teacher adds questions which scaffold the story for Sunny (lines 8, 9, 11). Sunny's answer to each question actually helps him to tell the story (lines 10, 12). Sunny's turns consist entirely of incomplete sentences, which the teacher extends.

Scaffolding of oral interactions by the teacher, whether for formal presentations or social interaction, is found not only in the early school years. In senior years, where students must also learn to develop their oral interaction skills for academic discourse, we find similar examples of scaffolding, as we'll see in later chapters.

Context and Oral Interaction

As we have described, oral interaction in education, and specifically within the classroom, may differ according to formality, but it may also vary according to the context—what type of classroom it is in (for example, ESL, foreign language class, or content-based), according to the different pedagogical approaches being used by the teacher, and even what is happening within different parts of the lesson. For instance, look at Classroom Snapshot 1.13. The ESL teacher is showing pictures of animals at the beach, the destination for a forthcoming class excursion. She is asking different students to provide the name of the animal picture she is holding.

Classroom Snapshot 1.13

1 **Student:** Octopus?
2 **Teacher:** No because an octopus has teeth.
3 **Student:** Jellyfish?

(Oliver & Mackey, 2003, p. 523) ■

You can see how the teacher is very meaning-focused and in particular is working hard to elicit the correct lexical item from the students. Contrast this to Classroom Snapshot 1.14. In this case, the learners are recounting a story that had been the focus of a number of class activities—hearing the story told, reading the story as a large shared book, dramatizing the story in groups, and drawing and sequencing pictures about the story. In this activity, the teacher was talking with her students about conventional beginnings and endings of stories.

Classroom Snapshot 1.14

1 **Student:**   One upon a time.
2 **Teacher:**   No we say once.
3 **Student:**   Once.

(Oliver & Mackey, 2003, p. 524)

In Classroom Snapshot 1.14, the teacher explicitly focuses on the form of the student's language, providing a correction to the student's use of the word 'one' instead of 'once'. Interesting, too, is the student's immediate **uptake**: she repeats the teacher's correction without the teacher requiring her to do so. From these examples we can see how the teacher and her students respond in different ways to language at different times within lessons.

BICS and CALP

In addition to the context, the characteristics of the lesson, such as the cognitive or linguistic demands, will also contribute to differences in the nature of the oral interaction. In many ways these cognitive and linguistic demands parallel the development of language proficiency. Cummins (2000) makes the useful distinction between **BICS**, Basic Interpersonal Communication Skills, and **CALP**, Cognitive Academic Language Proficiency. Both types of proficiency are important in school. BICS are the kind of general everyday listening and speaking skills that learners draw on in most of their interaction with others. Learners in second language and immersion contexts, who need to use the target language in everyday speech will, over time, develop strong skills in BICS for social needs. CALP is required to deal with academic demands of school, and this kind of proficiency develops over a longer period of time. Although students might be fluent in a second language, and easily able to operate socially, they may struggle in more formal academic contexts of oral interaction, for example, when giving a speech or presentation, providing a summary or recount, or taking part in a debate or discussion.

Consider the transcripts in Classroom Snapshot 1.15. In transcript 1, students do not have to think a great deal about what they need to say in response to the teacher. In transcript 2, a student grapples with the meaning of an unfamiliar word—showing her cognitive reflection by asking the teacher what is meant by the word.

Classroom Snapshot 1.15

1

1	**Teacher:**	Right did you put your name up the top and put the date?
2	**J:**	Yes, I'm finished
3	**Teacher:**	Are you finished? Good I just have to hear these people read.
4	**W:**	I'm finished.
5	**Teacher:**	And you've finished yours? I just have to collect it.

2

1 **Teacher:** Now this morning we're going to look at a new big book. Now our new big book comes from New Zealand and it's a Maori story.

2 **F:** Mary?

3 **Teacher:** No Maori. Maori are special people that come from New Zealand and this is the story.

(Oliver, 2009b, pp. 42, 44) ▮

Because it is interactive, the characteristics of the learners will also impact on the nature of the oral interaction that occurs in classroom discourse. For instance, newly arrived ESL learners will interact with their teachers in a very different way from those students who have been learning a language for a longer period of time. Newly arrived students may rely on **formulaic language**: a 'ready-made' phrase that the student has picked up and knows off by heart. In the following Classroom Snapshot 1.16, Yessara, a new arrival and her friend Roberta are chatting with the teacher. On the topic of broken arms, Yessara plunges into the conversation (line 7) by repeating the phrase 'I don't know' (in this case, meaning 'somebody I don't know'). The use of this phrase helps Yessara to take part in the conversation and gain the attention of the teacher. The teacher works hard to decipher her meaning, and this helps Yessara rephrase what she wants to say. How formulaic language contributes to acquisition is an area we will explore in greater detail in Chapter 2.

Classroom Snapshot 1.16

1 **Roberta:** I hope I get a broken arm and so does Amy.

2 **Teacher:** Yeah [daughter's name] wants a broken arm too so she can have some plaster.

3 **Yessara:** I don't know I don't know I don't know yeah I
I don't know my name little baby arm broken … little baby.

4 **Teacher:** When you were a little baby you had=

5 **Yessara:** No no no I don't know so so someone someone baby braken arm= they did.

6 **Teacher:**   Oh someone had a baby who had a broken arm?
7 **Yessara:**   Yeah.

(Philp & Duchesne, 2008, p. 98) ■

In contrast, learners who are further along their language acquisition journey (i.e. their interlanguage continuum) may respond more automatically or they may use the greater demands of the interaction as a trigger for processing new and more complex forms of the language. In Chapter 2 we will discuss the roles that **information processing** and **automaticity** play in language development.

Age of the Learners

Because of differences in their level of social-emotional and cognitive development, we also know that the age of the learners will contribute to differences in the type of oral interaction that occurs. For instance, it is hard to imagine an adult speaker—even one not proficient in the language—participating in the conversation between Binh and Theo in Classroom Snapshop 1.17.

Classroom Snapshot 1.17

1 **Binh:**   Red.
2 **Theo:**   Binh there's no red allowed to be on that.
3 **Binh:**   Gonna tell the teacher.
4 **Theo:**   Will you stop it … will you stop it … will you stop it right no:w.
              [singing in a funny voice to the tape recorder]

(Philp, Oliver, & Mackey, 2006, p. 561) ■

In future chapters we will consider the different ways that younger second language learners (Chapter 3) and older second language learners (Chapter 4) develop their oral interaction, and the factors that can impact upon this.

Summary

In this chapter, we have seen that oral interaction in the classroom can be between peers, and between teachers (or assistants) and students. These interactions can be for a variety of purposes and can be relatively informal and social, or be more formal and pedagogic. Oral interactions contain language that is different from written texts, and we have noted that it is important for second language development that learners develop oral literacy as well as print literacy. In the next chapter, we explore how the process of engaging in oral interaction can contribute to acquisition of new language as well as promoting fluency and more accurate use of language already known. We will see that a number of factors contribute to the success of this. Among these factors are the characteristics of the learners, including their age and the stage of development along with personality and affective factors, such as attitudes and motivation. In Chapter 1, we have also seen that oral interaction varies according to the classroom context, who is involved in the interaction, and what is occurring in the classroom at any given point. In Chapter 2, we will consider how interaction contributes to language learning and how it serves both linguistic and social functions in this process. As noted, in Chapters 3 and 4 we will explore interaction for primary- and high school-aged learners in more detail. In Chapter 5, we return to these key themes through revisiting common beliefs about oral interaction, and considering what second language research suggests about the potential of oral interaction for learning in the school context.

Activity 1.4

Look back at the Classroom Snapshots provided in this chapter. Find an example to illustrate each of the concepts or terms in the left-hand column. If you are unclear on the meaning of any term, see the Glossary at the end of the book.

Term	Classroom Snapshot / Line numbers
Negotiation	
Scaffolding	
BICS	
CALP	
Interaction for social purposes	
Interaction for academic purposes	
Collaboration	
Reciprocity	

Photocopiable © Oxford University Press

Table 1.1 Interaction terms and concepts

2

Oral Interaction: Purposes and Possibilities for Learning

Preview

As we outlined in Chapter 1, oral interaction is integral to learning a language. It is a vital part of what and how we teach: oral interaction contributes not only to language and literacy development, but also helps students learn the content of subject areas in mainstream classroom contexts. In Chapters 3 and 4, we will explore in greater detail the role of interaction for primary and high school students, particularly in their classrooms. To do this, we first need to understand more generally how interaction contributes to language learning, both through the cognitive processes within the individual learner and the social processes that shape language and thinking. We will also look at the importance of oral interaction in the social lives of children and adolescents learning a new language.

Linguistic Purposes: Learning Language by Using Language

Key Components of Language Learning and Teaching

According to Nation (2007, see also Nation & Newton, 2009), language learning and teaching should involve four key strands: **meaning-focused input**, **meaning-focused output**, **language-focused learning**, and **fluency development**. These are outlined in Figure 2.1 below. Nation identified these four elements through research about vocabulary learning and the recognition that learners need to focus on both language form and language use (see Lightbown 2013 for a discussion of the four strands in relation to content-based language teaching). Although they are here described separately in Figure 2.1, they often co-occur in classroom interaction. For the purposes of our book, we focus on speaking, but of course listening, reading, and writing would also promote these opportunities for learning. In this chapter, we explain the rationale behind these different aspects for teaching and learning in language classrooms.

	Meaning-focused input	Meaning-focused output	Language-focused learning	Fluency development
Learning opportunities	As learners strive to understand what is being said, they **notice** novel forms in the target language.	As learners strive to produce the target language and to be understood, they make connections between language form and meaning.	As learners deliberately pay attention to language features in the context of meaningful communication, they notice connections between language form and meaning.	As learners practice use of known language items and features, they become more automatic in their use.
Rationale from SLA theory	Krashen's **input hypothesis** (1985); Schmidt's **noticing hypothesis** (2001)	Swain's **output hypothesis** (1985; 1995) Long's Interaction Hypothesis (1996)	Schmidt's noticing hypothesis (2001)	DeKeyser (2007) on the importance of practice
Example	Listening to the teacher, learners make sense of novel words from context and non-linguistic cues for example, gesture, facial expression. (See Classroom Snapshot 2. 1.)	Talking during a pair-work task, a student may rephrase what they say in response to communication problems. (See Classroom Snapshot 2. 2.)	Talking together about how to express what they want to say, learners turn their attention to language form. (See Classroom Snapshot 2. 3.)	Applying their knowledge of language by putting it into practice. This slow process of matching forms with meanings gradually becomes faster and more automatic with practice. (See Classroom Activity 2. 1.)

Figure 2.1 Four strands of learning through listening and speaking (based on Nation, 2007; Nation & Newton, 2009)

The descriptions of these key components of a language classroom are very different from traditional approaches common before the 1970s including, for example, Grammar Translation. Although Grammar Translation is still much used today in some regions, particularly in foreign language contexts where language is taught as an academic subject rather than a skill, communicative language teaching approaches, with a focus on language use, rather than language form, are now more common.

Developments in Language Teaching

An emphasis on language use has emerged as a key development in English Language Teaching (ELT) and is consistent with changes that have occurred in theory about the nature of language and language competence. Specifically, the development of communicative language teaching (CLT) coincided with the recognition that competence in a language is more than just knowing the grammar rules. It also involves the ability to use language effectively (Hymes, 1972). The developments in the pedagogy of teaching English, and other languages, also reflect the changes that occurred regarding the goals of language learning, and the development of theories about second language acquisition (SLA). For descriptions of the history of English language teaching, see Celce-Murcia, 2001; Larsen-Freeman & Anderson, 2011; Richards & Rogers, 2001; for descriptions of theories of second language acquisition, see Lightbown & Spada, 2013; Van Patten & Williams, 2007.

Theories of Second Language Acquisition

Meaning-Focused Input

Influential in the 1980s—the early period of SLA research—was the work of Krashen who developed the Input Hypothesis. Krashen (1985) claimed that what is necessary and sufficient for language learning is comprehensible (meaningful) input (the first element—meaning-focused input—shown in Figure 2.1). Although few would disagree that comprehensible input is necessary for successful second language (L2) learning, many question whether it is enough (for example, Long, 1996; White, 1987). Yet even today there is a strong belief amongst some researchers and teachers that all language learners require for acquisition is abundant and understandable language 'input', either written or oral.

This need for understandable or comprehensible input as a tenet of language learning theory continues to have a considerable impact on pedagogy and even on the way language classrooms are organized. For instance, the focus on meaning is the foundation of CLT—a teaching approach that continues to influence many language teachers. The emphasis of this approach is on the communication of messages and meaning (Spada, 2007). Thus if you go into language classrooms, you often find teachers who are doing their utmost to provide abundant and meaningful input for students. In fact, language teachers sometimes go to extraordinary lengths to ensure that their students understand.

Teachers provide comprehensible input in many ways, including in the way they modify their own language when teaching. For example, in anticipation of, or in response to comprehension difficulties, teachers often clarify through elaboration, simplification, repetition, and reformulation. They ask questions to check comprehension and use body language, gesture, and facial expressions to accompany speech. (We will look some more at the ways that teachers talk in primary school language classrooms in Chapter 3.)

Consider Classroom Snapshot 2.1, another part of the lesson we looked at in Chapter 1 (Classroom Snapshot 1.15). See how the teacher uses repetition and questions as she attempts to make the input from the text she is reading meaningful to her students.

Classroom Snapshot 2.1

1	**Teacher:**	'She was a bony old woman, she had bony legs, and bony fingers and feathers on her bony arms.' What do I mean by bony? Pia?
2	**Student:**	Bones.
3	**Teacher:**	Right where are your bones? Feel your bones. [teacher touches her wrist, elbow, shoulder]
4	**Student:**	Here.
5	**Teacher:**	Good you can feel inside you've got bones.

(Oliver, 2009b, p. 44)

Teachers also attempt to make input comprehensible by using a variety of teaching resources. For example, they often give oral models and place written labels on classroom objects and provide concrete examples in the form of realia, pictures, and other media. Teachers develop resources that will assist in making input meaningful and they take students on excursions and invite visitors into their classrooms. Certainly teachers expend a great deal of effort to make sure their learners understand the input that they are getting in the classroom.

However, it is not only teachers and materials that enable input to become comprehensible to learners. Interaction between learners is also helpful in making the new language meaningful. That is, the process of *using language* can result in comprehensible input. This can occur as students chat with each other, be it about classroom content or other topics, or when they work on communication tasks or activities. For example, in Classroom Snapshot 1.5, we saw how one learner was able to make the term 'balancing' meaningful for her partner. Listen to your students working together and you will also be able to hear how learners work together to make meaning.

It is important to note, as do Nation & Newton (2009), that not all input is likely to be effective for learning. In order to learn something new, the learner must have some knowledge of most of the linguistic features in a given text (oral or written) already. Meaningful input is effective when, through the potential assistance of context, shared knowledge, and/or nonlinguistic cues, learners are able to make sense of the rest. Krashen proposed the term 'i +1' as a way to characterize input that is comprehensible to learners, containing not only vocabulary but also grammatical features that are a little beyond their current interlanguage. In this way, development is possible.

Another view on how input becomes comprehensible comes from Long (1996) who argues that as learners engage in interaction, and particularly as they negotiate for meaning, input becomes comprehensible and thus available for acquisition. A variety of contexts have been described to support the position that interaction is needed, the most memorable being case studies showing the difficulties that hearing children of deaf parents have encountered acquiring spoken language from language heard on television (Sachs, Bard, & Johnson, 1981): a context that does not provide opportunities for interaction. Therefore, researchers now contend that other elements are also necessary for second language learning to occur. One such element (the second shown in Figure 2.1) is output: learners need opportunities to produce the new language they are learning (i.e. the target language).

Meaning-Focused Output

In 1985, based on her observation of immersion classes in Canada, Swain proposed the Output Hypothesis. In this she suggested that it is through the process of actually producing the target language themselves—saying what they want to say—that learners acquire language. Swain (1985, 1995) specifies three important functions of output: noticing, hypothesizing, and reflecting. For example, in a study of school-aged immersion students working on a collaborative writing activity (i.e. a **dictogloss**), Kowal & Swain (1994) found that the output the learners produced helped them to notice the gaps in their knowledge and to link the form of the language (such as the grammar, syntax, or even the morphology of words) with its function (or purpose) and its meaning. It also provided them with opportunities to test their hypotheses about the target language, that is, to try out new language forms and get feedback on what they produced. Finally, learners in the upper years of primary school and at **secondary school** may use their **metalinguistic** knowledge to reflect on and solve problems they encounter in their production. This often occurs when learners work collaboratively.

Activity 2.1

Look at the following conversation between two low proficiency learners of Italian, from a high school class. Complete Table 2.1 by identifying the linguistic problems they encounter and by indicating whether and how they are solved. Then consider the three questions that appear after the table.

Lesson: Recipe Task

In this activity the learners are describing a recipe.

 1 **Student I:** Why is it why is it *il* or *la*? I don't understand it.
 2 **Student K:** Because it ends in 'a' it's *la* and 'o' it's *il*.
 3 **Student I:** Oh I get it. *Grattugiano … grattugiano il cioccolato.* [correct stress the second time] No how do you say 'smash' *le uove*?
 4 **Student K:** Break.
 5 **Student I:** Break, break. [trying to find the word in dictionary]
 6 **Student K:** We'll have no break. Mix the cream and eggs.
 7 **Student I:** *Mescoli.* [You mix.]
 8 **Student K:** *Non.*
 9 **Student I:** *Mescolano.* [stress in wrong place] [They mix.]
10 **Student K:** *Mescolano.*
11 **Student I:** *Mescolano il crema.* [They mix the cream.]
12 **Student K:** *La*=
13 **Student I:** =*Crema* is *o*. If I have *o* its *crema*=
14 **Student K:** =No.

(Tognini, 2008, pp. 243–4)

Lines	Problem	Assistance	Resolution
1–3	Student I Choosing the correct article (masculine or feminine)	Student K	✓ Student I applies rule *il cioccolato* (**target like** use)
3–6	Student I Word for 'smash'	Student K Suggests a different word	Searches word for 'break' (unsuccessful)
4–6	Student I Word for 'break'	Student I Uses dictionary	
7–11	Student I Verb form *mescolare* (to mix) (target = *mescolate*)		
12–14			

Photocopiable © Oxford University Press

Table 2.1 Linguistic problems in a cooking lesson

1 How does their conversation reflect the difficulties these students are having in making connections between what they mean and how to say it (form)?

2 Do you see an example of these students using their metalinguistic knowledge to help them solve their difficulty? Does it solve or add to the problem?

3 What is the contribution of each learner in this collaborative effort?

Activity 2.1 shows how, through collaboration, learners are able to resolve some of the impasses that occur in their interaction (that is, they have engaged in meaning-focused output and language-focused learning as described in Figure 2.1). Through the feedback they provide to each other they ultimately produce language in a form that moves towards being more grammatical and meaningful. In this way, producing **comprehensible output** works to move learners along their personal interlanguage continuum. García Mayo (2002) explains that this can occur because as learners produce output, especially in collaborative ways, their attention is drawn to 'those parts of their interlanguage that deviate from the target language or on forms that are not yet in the learners' interlanguage repertoire' (p. 325).

This can be observed in Classroom Snapshot 2.2.

Classroom Snapshot 2.2

1 **NNS1:**   Where is the= the where is the [life] go?
2 **NNS2:**   … What you say?
3 **NNS1:**   The [life].
4 **NNS2:**   The life?
5 **NNS1:**   The b[r]ead knife.

(Oliver, 1998, p. 378) ∎

In the first line, the student (NNS1) pronounces the word 'knife' incorrectly; in subsequent turns and in response to feedback from her partner (NNS2), she attempts to adjust her output. Hence, by producing output the learner's awareness is heightened, not only in terms of her own production, but also about what is required in the target language. It has been suggested that as learners make attempts to produce the target language, and interact with others, they become aware. As Schmidt (1990) describes it, they notice the gap between what they produce and the target language form. It is this noticing that supports language acquisition because it draws learners' attention to connections between the use of a particular form and its meaning. This is reflected in a study by Philp & Iwashita (2013) with adult learners of French. They compared pairs of learners who interacted on communicative tasks with pairs who simply observed others carrying out the same task. In interviews following these tasks, those who observed the interaction made more comments reflecting empathy for the speakers, feeling sorry for the difficulty one learner was having in trying to express himself, or admiring the patience of the other learner: 'I think it was great how she was trying to help him explain what he was saying' (p. 14). However, those involved directly in the interaction made more remarks about the language itself, and the choices they struggled to make when expressing themselves: 'I wanted to say … "everyone panicked and they all fell"… I knew that I had to use um *avoir* with the participe *passé* and um être and the participe *passé* so I kinda got them mixed around especially because um *sont* and *ont* sounded um s … kind of have the same sound so I kind of got the two verbs mixed up I think it worked out in the end though' (p. 17). This supports Swain's assertion that having to produce language leads learners to notice language form.

Thus, a significant aspect of comprehensible output is the active engagement of the learners. That is, by producing language a little beyond language that is easy for them, or as Swain (1985) describes it, **pushed output**, learners are fully involved in connecting language forms to meaning. They are not just observing the language or responding by rote, the way children can recite their times tables looking out the classroom window. Instead they are actively engaging with and using language. That is, they have to work out how the target language system 'works' when they need it to express what they want to say and when they want to make sense to others.

Fluency Development

By using language, learners also gain practice in the target language and in doing this, they increase their fluency in the use of the language (the fourth element of Figure 2.1). This is not practice as reflected in the type of drills some of us may have endured learning a foreign language, the type that can be performed without any thought. Rather, it is the type of practice DeKeyser (2007) describes when learners are given the opportunity to develop new skills, greater fluency, and automaticity in their second language through meaningful interaction. The benefit of practice is that as learners gain more skill, they require less effort to produce language and become more fluent (Segalowitz, 2003). Ultimately, their responses become more automatic or, as Gass (2013) says, more 'fast, unconscious, and effortless' (p. 231).

Automaticity plays an important role in the acquisition of a language, because it allows attention to be freed up. Initially, the beginning language learner finds everything an effort when speaking the target language. Even a simple sentence is difficult to create because every aspect of it requires conscious effort. Apart from formulaic chunks, speech is halting as the learner must think about every single word and morpheme. This is true of all learning—can you remember when you first learned to ride a bike, or drive a car, or play an instrument? It was painfully slow and all-consuming. This is because new skills require our full attention. With practice, however, it becomes less demanding. Just in the way that a skilled driver, cyclist, or musician can perform the task and carry on a conversation at the same time, with hours of practice, language performance also becomes automatic— that is, ultimately, it no longer requires conscious attention.

Language-Focused Learning

This development of automaticity is part of a long process in language acquisition and has been described by some researchers as occurring in stages, and involving different types of knowledge and/or processing. Specifically, researchers make a distinction between the kind of explicit **declarative knowledge** that learners first have about a skill, for example, learning the steps in how to tie a shoelace, with the **procedural knowledge** they develop as they come to carry out an action or skill with ease, for example, tying one's shoelace without thinking about it (Anderson, 1983; Muranoi, 2007). In language we can compare, for example, the need for a beginner learner to remind herself to put an 's' on the end of noun that is plural (declarative knowledge), with her later growing ability to consistently use 's' to mark plural without referring to the rule (procedural knowledge). This occurs with practice over time until ultimately, she is able to do this fluently and automatically, without thinking. What is key to our discussion about how language learning occurs is that language classrooms can prepare learners by providing practice in the target language that helps them expand their knowledge of the language and develop fluency in using it. When such practice time is restricted, as for example in many foreign language classrooms, successful language learning is more difficult to achieve.

So far we have seen that comprehensible input (understanding) and comprehensible output (production), and the associated noticing and practice lead to eventual fluency and automaticity. We have also seen the importance of what Nation (see Figure 2.1) refers to as language-focused learning and others refer to as **form focus** (Long, 1988), that is, the opportunity to attend to language features in the context of meaningful communication. In Nation's four-strand model, some instructional activities may put the focus on features of the language itself, but the features of language that are studied in these activities are always chosen from those that will be useful when students go back to the meaning-focused activities, not from a list drawn from a grammar book. Together, all these elements develop through interaction and then, working in concert, they facilitate language learning.

From most of the snapshots we have viewed so far it would seem that oral interactions, in the main, go along quite smoothly. However, as we all know too well, this is not always the case. Misunderstanding does occur in conversations and it can lead to communication breakdown between speakers, be they proficient language users or learners of the language. Based on what we have argued so far, it is logical to conclude that this could be problematic for learners—if only because there is a lack of comprehensible input being received and a reduction in comprehensible output being produced. However, for some time now it has been claimed that the process of working to overcome the breakdown actually makes positive contributions to language learning (Long, 1988).

Contribution of Negotiation for Meaning

As indicated in Chapter 1, the type of spoken exchanges that occurs when there is communication breakdown, and especially the efforts that are made to overcome this, is labeled 'negotiation for meaning' (NFM) or 'negotiated interaction' (for example, Oliver, 1998, 2000, 2002; Philp, Adams, & Iwashita, 2013; Pica, 1994, 2013). Such interaction occurs in response to communication difficulties and speakers adjust their speech in different ways to try to gain mutual understandings. This includes the use of such strategies as repetition, confirmation checks, clarification requests, reformulation, and comprehension checks.

Because negotiated interaction does appear to promote conditions that facilitate language learning (for example, comprehensible input, comprehensible output, noticing), over the years there has been a considerable body of research investigating the conditions that promote its occurrence, as well as the factors that influence these and how negotiation (and other forms of feedback) assist language learners. For some time most of these studies were conducted with adults, but this began to change in the 1990s with a number of studies about children negotiating for meaning. One such study is described in Spotlight Study 2.1.

Spotlight Study 2.1

Oliver (2002) examined the interaction of 96 age- and gender-matched pairs of children aged 8–13 years. The pairs were organized so that ESL learners were paired with either English-only speaking children (NS) or with other learners, and done so according to how proficient they were at speaking English (i.e. high or low proficiency). To serve as point of comparison, there were also 16 pairs of English-only speaking children. In the different groups there were an equal number of male–male and female–female pairs in each. For example, of 16 high proficiency-NS pairs, eight were male and eight were female. Similarly there were an equal number of younger (8–10 years) and older (11–13 years) learners in each group.

The pairs were audio- and video-recorded as they worked on two communication tasks. These interactions were transcribed and then examined for features of negotiation for meaning. The results for each grouping were then compared.

Oliver found that there were significant differences between the pairings according to whether they included English-only or ESL learners. For example, English-only language speakers when paired together (NS–NS) negotiated for meaning much less often than did pairs that included at least one ESL learner

(NS–NNS or NNS–NNS). ESL learners also were more likely to tolerate ambiguity when working on the tasks and, as a consequence and somewhat surprisingly, the English-only students took much longer to complete each task because they sought to achieve a level of precision that the learners seemed less concerned about or less able to achieve.

The pairs also varied significantly according to the proficiency level of the learners. For example, ESL learners negotiated less often as their proficiency increased, so that when high proficiency learners were paired together they negotiated less often than did pairs made up of a high–low proficiency grouping, who in turn negotiated less than did the low–low pairing. There were no differences observed according to age or gender of the pairings.

Overall, the results show that child ESL learners use a range of negotiation for meaning strategies (see Snapshot 2.3 and 2.4) leading to the conclusion that 'peers are an important source of data about the target language and that the use of peers in teaching practices [is] justified in a primary school setting' (p. 108). ▪

As in many other studies, the type of negotiation strategies identified in Spotlight study 2.1 included those in the form of repetition, confirmation checks, and clarification requests. These usually involve the listener working to make sense of the output of their partner. This is illustrated below using the same exchange as shown in Chapter 1 (Classroom Snapshot 1.6), as partner Frederique seeks to clarify what My Phoung said and to confirm this.

Classroom Snapshot 2.3

1	**My Phoung:**	It's a= one tree. One tree.	
2	**Frederique:**	What?	← Clarification request
3	**My Phoung:**	One tree.	
4	**Frederique:**	One tree?	← Confirmation check (with repetition)
5	**My Phoung:**	Yeah.	
6	**Frederique:**	One tree.	
7	**My Phoung:**	In the=	
8	**Frederique:**	=What one t[h]ree mean?	← Clarification request
9	**My Phoung:**	Tree.	
10	**Frederique:**	One tree!	← Repetition
11	**My Phoung:**	Yes tree. Tree.	← Repetition

(Oliver, 2002, p. 98) ▪

In contrast, speakers use comprehension checks (sometimes also involving repetition and reformulation) to ascertain that their partner understands what they are attempting to say. You will see in Classroom Snapshot 2.4, when Ho is describing a kitchen scene as part of a communication game, she checks that her partner follows her meaning. This is particularly pertinent in this exchange as she does not use the word 'drawers' as expected, but instead uses the word 'tray'—a word often used by Australian teachers to describe the single and removable drawer students have under their desks. After Ho checks, her partner Min indicates that she does understand.

Classroom Snapshot 2.4

1	**Ho:**	And they have a cupboard.
2		Cupboard like that.	← Repetition
3		And a tray.
4		They have a tray you know?	← Comprehension check
5		One two three.
6		Three tray.	← Reformulation
7		Tray.	← Repetition
8		Know what tray?	← Comprehension check
9		Three tray.
10	**Min:**	Yer yer I know.

(Oliver, 2002, p. 98) ■

As has been illustrated in this and previous snapshots, negotiated interaction serves a variety of purposes. Repetition, for instance, gives speakers a 'second look' at the input and helps make input more meaningful. Clarification requests can work in the same way, and in fact, often do result in repetition, but in addition with the form and/or meaning clarified for the listener. Through negotiation, input is made more comprehensible— some say this leads to vocabulary acquisition and greater phonological accuracy (Ellis, Tanaka, & Yamazaki, 1994; Nation & Laufer, 2012). In addition, as learners are forced to manipulate their output in ways that make it more comprehensible for their partner, negotiation strategies encourage participation in the conversation, for instance, indicating to those in the conversation when it is their turn to respond (Scarcella & Higa, 1981). Negotiated interaction also directs participants' attention within the conversation as is it helps them to notice the problematic or confusing part of what has been said. When what they produce is not clear, they receive immediate feedback as in Classroom Snapshot 2.5.

Classroom Snapshot 2.5

1	**NS:**	Where do you put the saucepan?
2	**NNS:**	Saucepan? … Um under the= the first to cook … the food.
3	**NS:**	Under the cooker?
4	**NNS:**	Yep.
5	**NS:**	On the floor?
6	**NNS:**	No. In the cooker. On the cooker.

(Oliver, 1995a, p. 476) ▨

As learners struggle to make themselves understood, the corrective feedback they receive helps them notice problems in their production and, as a result, destabilizes their interlanguage. In this case, the learner can compare and then use the word she was looking for ('cooker') with the phrase she initially uses ('the first to cook'). Long (1996, pp. 451–2) explains it this way, suggesting that the feedback learners get through conversational adjustments 'connects input, internal learner capacities, particularly selective attention, and output in productive ways'.

Corrective Feedback

The conversational strategies used during negotiation for meaning are just one type of conversational or interactional corrective feedback (Long, 1996). A variety of other forms have also been the focus of a great deal of research since the 1980s. For example, feedback may be provided more explicitly (as in Classroom Snapshot 1.14) and may be accompanied by different types of extrinsic reinforcement or enhancement—such as the use of paralinguistic cues (for example, raised eyebrows), a raised tone of voice to emphasize a correction, or by extended wait time when expecting a response.

Corrective feedback may also be in the form of metalinguistic comment, for example, in a French class for secondary students, the teacher corrects the student's pronunciation of 'dessert' ('desert'), and explicitly draws her attention to the meaning of the two pronunciations.

Classroom Snapshot 2.6

1	**Teacher:**	*Oui c'est ca. Plat principal. Et pour finir qu'est-ce qu'on mange pour finir? Le gâteau or des fruits?* [Yes that's it. The main course. And to end the meal what does one eat to finish the meal? Cake or fruit?]
2	**Student:**	*Le gâteau.* [The cake.]
3	**Teacher:**	*Oui ils s'appellent comment? Ils s'appellent comment?* [Yes what is that called? It's called?]

4 **Student:**   *Dessert* [English pronunciation]
5 **Teacher:**   *Le dessert oui.* [writes on board] *Le dessert. Attention de ne pas dire
                 'désert' parce que le 'désert' c'est comme le Sahara. OK? Le dessert.
                 Bon.* [Dessert yes. Dessert. Be careful not to say 'desert' because
                 'desert' is like the Sahara. OK? Dessert. Good.]

(Tognini, 2008, p. 151) ▣

In this example, the teacher first uses a **recast** (line 6), where she reformulates what the student has said, but with target like pronunciation, and use of the article. Hence, recasts are another form of corrective feedback and they are often prevalent in teacher language. A considerable amount of research has focused on recasts and for this reason we discuss this type of corrective feedback in greater detail below.

Recasts

Originally described in first language acquisition research (for example, Baker & Nelson, 1984; Farrar, 1990; Saxton, 1997), recasts provide feedback in such a way that the speaker's meaning is maintained but the form is corrected/reformulated and provided as a model.

Classroom Snapshot 2.7

1 **Learner:**   A [c]lower tree.
2 **NS:**   A flower tree.   ← Recast

(Oliver, 1995a, p. 472) ▣

It has been suggested that recasts are especially effective because the meaning conveyed in the feedback is closely tied with what learners are trying to say. Thus they can focus on the form of the language, rather than having to struggle with the form and the meaning at the same time, making it an easier task for them. It is thought that recasts also offer a direct contrast between what is in the target language and what the learner is producing, assisting learners to notice the gap and therefore facilitating their acquisition of language (Long, 2007).

   A number of studies, particularly those undertaken with language learners working in pairs, suggest that recasts are well used by learners. Specifically, what they produce after the recast (such as in Classroom Snapshot 2.5, 2.6, and 2.7) shows they often take up such feedback, using it and altering their production in the process (for example, Mackey & Philp, 1998; Oliver, 1995a, 2000). Further, as Mackey & Philp showed for adult learners, and Mackey & Oliver (2002) showed for child second language learners, such feedback can result in learning both in the short and, more importantly, in the long term. This depends however, on a number of factors, including the nature of the linguistic form (for example, Loewen & Philp, 2006), the context, and the nature of the recast (for example, Lyster & Mori, 2006), as we discuss below.

Although some classroom studies suggest that recasts may be beneficial for learners (for example, Tognini, 2008; Oliver, 2000), others, particularly Lyster and colleagues (for example, Lyster, 1998a & b; Lyster & Ranta, 1997) in the context of French immersion instruction, suggest that when recasts are not explicit, they may be ambiguous and confusing for learners. However, in the foreign language context of Japanese immersion, Lyster & Mori (2006) found that learners tended to identify recasts as corrective, and to make use of them. Lyster & Mori were able to explain these differences by taking a closer look at the overall instruction provided in these different immersion programs. They found that the instruction in the Japanese immersion classes was heavily oriented to form and accuracy. Thus, learners expected all types of teacher feedback, including recasts, to be corrective in nature. In the French immersion classrooms, however, the general orientation was on meaning and on content and thus students did not perceive less direct/overt teacher feedback as corrective, instead they tended to interpret recasts as reactions to the content rather than the form of what they said.

Therefore, Lyster & Mori (2006) suggest that the type of instruction, whether it is more oriented to content or to language, affects learners' perceptions of feedback. Similarly the type of learner can affect teachers' choices of the kind of feedback they use, as can the type of activity and what happens within the lesson:

1   Type of language classroom
    If the classroom is more language-focused than content-focused, the teacher might provide feedback that emphasizes language production and fluency and, as a consequence, provide recasts so as to cause the least disruption to the students' output practice. If the classroom is more concerned with content, the teacher might use negotiation strategies (for example, 'What do you mean?' 'Do you understand?') to ensure the learners develop understanding.

2   Type of language learners
    Some researchers suggest that teacher feedback will differ according to the learners' age (Oliver, 2000), or according to the learners' level

of proficiency (Philp, 2003). For example, Oliver found that teachers were more likely to provide feedback to adult learners than to child learners, and that the feedback to adults would be in the form of negotiation for meaning.

3 Type of language focus
   Another aspect that will affect the type of feedback teachers provide is the nature of the activity they set for their students. For example, the type of linguistic structure elicited in the task is important (for example, Doughty & Varela, 1998; Loewen & Philp, 2006), as some forms are best dealt with through explicit instruction, others through modeling or by negotiation (DeKeyser, 2005; Ellis, 2006).

4 Type of activity
   Finally, the feedback that is provided may differ according to what is happening within the lesson (for example, Ellis, Basturkmen, & Loewen, 2001; Oliver & Mackey, 2003; Lyster & Mori, 2006). For example, Oliver & Mackey (2003) found that teachers are more likely to provide explicit feedback during a language-focused aspect of the lesson, but will negotiate with the students when there is a more communicative focus.

There is still a lot more research to do before we really understand how useful recasts or other types of feedback may be within our classrooms. Even so, we do know that feedback is an integral part of the whole process of oral interaction. Further, research suggests this is true for different domains of language. Specifically, feedback has been found to provide opportunities for second language learners to develop and correct different aspects of their interlanguage. For example, it has been found to be beneficial for pronunciation (for example, Gass, 2003), for vocabulary (de la Fuente, 2002; Dobinson, 2001; Fountas & Pinnell, 2001; Gass, 2003; Genishi & Dyson, 1984; Shahraki & Kassaian, 2011) and grammar (Celce-Murcia, 1991; Ellis, 2006; Spada & Lightbown, 2008). One study that examined the acquisition of grammar is described in Spotlight Study 2.2.

Spotlight Study 2.2

Mackey & Oliver (2002) studied the development of English question forms by children aged 8–12 years who were enrolled at a school with an Intensive English Centre where there were a large number of low English proficiency ESL students from a wide range of language and cultural backgrounds. On return of the parental permission forms, 22 volunteer participants were selected and randomly assigned to two groups: one in which learners received interactional feedback from a native-speaking adult (treatment group), and another that did not (control group).

A number of communication tasks were designed for this study. They were based on familiar classroom materials and were similar to those used in a number of other studies (for example, Oliver, 2000, 2002). They included 'Spot the Difference', story completion, picture placement, and picture sequencing tasks and each was designed to elicit a range of different question forms.

According to previous research (Pienemann & Johnston, 1987) questions that students produce as they become more proficient in their second language, in this case English, can be sequenced in a developmental order. That is, there is an order of acquisition that seems to be based on how difficult the structures within each question are for learners to process. For instance, formulaic and unprocessed questions (for example, 'Hello, how are you?') are stage one questions; questions with a subject-verb-object order (for example, 'She is big?') are stage two questions; whereas 'Wh-' and 'Do-' questions (for example, 'What the girl say?' 'Do you have a dog?') are stage three questions. Stage four (for example, 'Have you got a boy holding a stick?') and then stage five questions (for example, 'What have you got in the sky?') become increasing more difficult structurally. (See Lightbown & Spada, 2013, for a more detailed description of the stages of question formation, examples, and research.)

Prior to participating in the activities that were designed for the study, the students were pretested to determine their level of question development (i.e. which stage 1, 2, 3, etc.). Next, the tasks were undertaken with an adult in a one-on-one situation for approximately 30 minutes for three consecutive days. The students in the treatment group were provided with interactional feedback, specifically using negotiation strategies or recasts, whenever a question they produced was problematic. For example:

Learner: The three fall down? Three little ones
Researcher: Did three little ones fall down? ← Recast & comprehension check

In contrast, those in the control group did not receive this type of feedback. For example:

Learner: There's a boy ... dad showing boy like aeropolane?
Researcher: Oh OK. I've got a dad and a son but my dad has his hands in his pockets.

The next day after the intervention, a post-test was held, as was another one week later and another three weeks from the intervention.

The results showed that immediately after the intervention most of the 11 children in the treatment group improved and nine of these children went on to maintain at least one stage increase in their development in later post-tests. In contrast, only three of the 11 control group children improved in the same period of time. These results were interpreted as support for the claim that interaction supports second language acquisition. Interestingly, when compared to similar studies with adult learners (for example, Mackey & Philp, 1998) it appears 'children's interlanguage seemed to be impacted by feedback relatively quickly' (Mackey & Oliver, 2002, p. 459). ■

Furthermore, as has been found in the first language context (for example, Clay, 2001; Hay & Fielding-Barnsley, 2009; Snow, Griffin, & Burns, 2005) oral interaction, including the provision of feedback, strongly supports the development of writing for second language learners (Genishi & Dyson, 1984). In fact, as we discuss in Chapter 3, some go as far as to suggest that interaction is the very foundation of writing development, especially for intermediate students (Fountas & Pinnell, 2001). Sadly, some teachers fail · to recognize the importance of oral work and provide limited opportunities for students to interact in class.

Review

In this section we have described key features of oral interaction in the language classroom. Based on theories of second language acquisition, we considered four main experiences in language classrooms that are important for second language learning: meaning-focused input; meaning-focused output; language-focused learning; and fluency activities that promote automaticity. We have also outlined ways in which features and functions of oral interaction support language development. We emphasized the need for learners to try out language forms during meaningful communication, to reflect on language, and to develop greater automaticity in language use. We noted that feedback provided by the teacher or peers plays an integral part in this process. Finally we noted that interaction is important not only for oral language learning, but also for developing print literacy.

Social Nature of Learning

Collaboration

So far in this chapter, we have concentrated on the interaction between teachers and students from a cognitive perspective, where the emphasis is on the individual's response within oral interactions. Another way of understanding the contribution of oral interaction for learning is from a sociocultural perspective. In this view, development does not just occur in the mind of the individual learner, but it is something that happens in the context of interaction. For example, in a revised version of the output hypothesis, Swain (2005) highlights collaboration between learners as a source of language development. As learners work together on activities that push them to express themselves clearly in the target language, they help one another progress in their language production and to stretch their linguistic abilities. This is seen in the following example of two learners, Patrick and Joseph, in a primary school classroom, creating a sign for a platypus enclosure. They work out together how to express what they want to say. They draw from their collective knowledge and try out different possible forms to use. As Gibbons (1991, p. 28) points out, what they eventually come up with is something that probably neither of them would have achieved on their own. The children incorporate one another's suggestions, in terms of both content and language. For example, Patrick initially uses the word 'spine' (line 2), but he later adopts the correct term 'spur' (line 6), following Joseph's use of it in the previous turn. Through collaboration, their language becomes more precise and more complex.

Classroom Snapshot 2.8

1 **Joseph:**   So … if we have a sign that says … if you find a platypus take it … take him to … a … no … a staff member.

2 **Patrick:** No, no … don't touch it … please don't touch … yes yes that's what we'll do … we'll put … please don't … no … please don't touch platypus spine.

3 **Joseph:**   No … what is it? … what is it? … it's got something that's poisonous.

4 **Patrick:** So that'll make the people walk away … because they aren't going to take it home if it's got something poisonous on it.

5 **Joseph:**   Please … please don't touch the platypus because it has … a poisonous spur.

6 **Patrick:** Yes … please do not touch the platypus because of its spur … its spur is dangerous and you will have to be taken to hospital … right?

(Gibbons, 1991, pp. 27–8) ■

Within the field of educational psychology this idea, originally applied to children's cognitive development, is referred to as 'social constructivism' (Duchesne et al., 2013). The social nature of learning is emphasized, and classroom activities are often centered around peer group-work. Learners are active participants in the learning process and it is the actual process of relating to others that shapes the way they think and the things they do. Some applied linguists, such as Swain (2010) and Gibbons (2006), influenced by Vygotsky's work (1978), have applied these same ideas to second language learning. One key part of this is the idea of scaffolding (Wood, Bruner, & Ross, 1976). This term is borrowed from the image of a building scaffold—a framework that provides support during construction and shows the shape of the future building. Once the building is complete, the scaffolding is no longer necessary: the building stands alone. Applied to language learning, you can imagine the help provided by an expert adult or peer as a kind of scaffold that enables learners to carry out a task that is beyond their capacity to complete on their own.

Different Ways of Scaffolding Learning

Teacher Scaffolding

Scaffolding can involve different types of strategies, including helping a child maintain focus or to keep trying. In language classrooms, teachers often provide scaffolding through co-construction and by models. In Classroom Snapshot 2.9, as the child attempts to recount an event, the teacher's questions serve as a scaffold, helping him to describe what happened. We saw a similar example in Classroom Snapshot 1.19. For young children, as seen here, the teacher's scaffold not only assists with language production, but also helps the child to structure the recounting of the story itself.

Classroom Snapshot 2.9

1 **Teacher:**   What did you do in the garden?
2 **Student:**   Mm cut the tree.
3 **Teacher:**   You cut the trees. Were they big trees or were they little bushes?
4 **Student:**   Big trees.
5 **Teacher:**   How did you cut them?
6 **Student:**   What?
7 **Teacher:**   How did you cut them? Did you have a big knife?
8 **Student:**   You know big knife?

(Oliver, 2000, p. 140)

Other researchers have argued that learners may use their L1 as a scaffold, to think through a difficult task, and to make sense of grammar in the L2 or to fill in for missing L2 words when proficiency is very low (for example, Alegría & García Mayo, 2009; Brooks, Donato, & McGlone, 1997; Mori, 2004). We will return to this issue in Chapter 3.

A key aspect of scaffolding that is central to Vygotsky's theory of learning is the Zone of Proximal Development (ZPD). This describes the range of potential between what learners are able to do alone unassisted, and what they are enabled to accomplish with the assistance of an expert. In the case of language learning, this 'expert' could be an adult or a more capable peer, that is, a conversational partner whose linguistic proficiency is greater than the learner's. This assisted performance is a precursor to what the learner will eventually be able to accomplish independently. Applied to language development rather than cognitive development, the ZPD is often used to describe progress in language use, frequently achieved through the use of scaffolding. Progress is shown when less scaffolding is required.

This is demonstrated in Classroom Snapshot 2.10, again from research by Gibbons (2006). Following a science experiment with year 5-learners (aged 9–11 years) the teacher models the appropriate language for reporting the results. Here, the students are learning to generalize their findings. Instead of talking about a single thumbtack, they use the plural form to suggest that all thumbtacks are attracted to magnets. Notice how the teacher in this example gradually reduces the amount of explicit instruction and modeling to the students as they become more adept with expressing the results scientifically.

Classroom Snapshot 2.10

1	**Teacher:**	Right now we're going to talk about all thumbtacks. So we're going to talk about magnets … Try it this way. Magnets=
2	**Student:**	=Attract thumbtacks.
3	**Teacher:**	=Attract thumbtacks=Let's try it.
4	**Student:**	Magnets attract thumbtacks.
5	**Teacher:**	Remember I'm not talking about just one I'm talking about all magnets. I'm talking about all thumbtacks so let's try it again.
6	**Student:**	Magnets attract thumbtacks.
7	**Teacher:**	The nail is magnetic … so you tell me.
8	**Student:**	The nail=
9	**Teacher:**	=Magnets=
10	**Student:**	Magnets attract the nail. The nails.
11	**Teacher:**	Again.
12	**Student:**	Magnets attract nails.
13	**Teacher:**	That's hard … this paper clip. Remember the steel paper clips are magnetic.
14	**Student:**	Magnets attract steel paper clips.

(Gibbons, 2006, p. 133) ■

Here the collaborative interaction between the students and the expert interlocutor (i.e. the teacher) reflects a growing ability for the students to express themselves scientifically. Although they are initially unable to use language in this way, this joint dialogue is a precursor to what they will soon be able to do unassisted, and they will be able to apply the principle to other forms.

Activity 2.2

Look again at the transcript we saw in Chapter 1 (Activity 1.3, Lesson 2) from a primary class for new arrivals. One child is selected to tell the class which part of a story he liked the best. Some of the ways in which the teacher scaffolds the child's performance have been highlighted in bold. For each one, explain how it scaffolds the child's ability to do the task. Write your answers in Table 2.2. The first one is done for you. When you have finished, look back at Chapter 1 to compare your answers with the description given there of scaffolding.

1	**Teacher:**	What is your favorite part?
2	**Student:**	I like Riding Hood once upon a time.
3	**Teacher:**	Yeah what part of the story do you like the best= do you like the best?
4		Can you= you can remember the story can't you?
5	**Student:**	One.
6	**Teacher:**	**Um Yiqian go and get me the little book over there.**
7	**Student:**	The Red Riding=
8	**Teacher:**	**Yeah the Red Riding Hood.**
9	**Student:**	XX.
10	**Teacher:**	Shh [quietens children]
11		The little books
12		OK here's the little books
13	**Teacher:**	**Select a picture. Select a picture or select a part of the story that you like**> Sh [quietens other children] **OK now what was the story. Show the picture. Now what was the stor= what was that part of the story?**
14	**Student:**	XX apple pie on the wolf.
15	**Teacher:**	Right [OK] hit the wolf with what?
16	**Student:**	Apple pie.
17	**Teacher:**	With an apple pie. **With a plate and had an apple pie on it. Right where did the wolf go from there?** When he hit the wolf= when Red riding hit the wolf with an apple pie where did the wolf go to?
18	**Student:**	Went to skateboard.

19	**Teacher:**	**Went to where the skateboard was and then what happened to the wolf?**
20	**Student:**	The wolf er out.
21	**Teacher:**	**Out of the window.**

(Mackey, Oliver, & Leeman, unpublished data)

Line	Scaffold	Comment
6	Actual book given to child	Pictures help child to remember parts of the story before having to talk about it
8		
13		
17		
19		
21		

Photocopiable © Oxford University Press

Table 2.2 Talking about a shared reading

Peer Scaffolding

Vygotskyian theorists emphasize the asymmetrical nature of the collaboration between novice and expert (Duchesne et al., 2013), but this notion of the ZPD and of scaffolding has also been used to describe processes of second language learning through collaboration between language learners (whether asymmetrical or symmetrical in level of proficiency) (Lantolf & Thorne, 2006). This is important for understanding a potential benefit of peer interaction: it suggests that even if learners are unable to correct one another with the confidence, skill, and accuracy of the teacher, they can provide one another with a sounding board and supported effort in puzzling over language problems—something Swain (2010) refers to as **languaging**. Philp, Adams, & Iwashita (2013) argue that it is the relatively symmetrical relationship between peers that offers the possibility to experiment, make mistakes, and try solutions (see Hartup 1989; Philp & Duchesne, 2008) and simply to enjoy language learning. This is illustrated in the following quote from a high school student, talking about her favorite activity in her French class, 'making up our own dialogues':

> *When you're working with your partner, you don't care about being silly …
> like (laughter from other students) when you say the wrong thing, or like
> you try to make up a word of your own that you think is in French and like,
> you just have fun with your partner. You don't have to be so serious.*

(Tognini, 2008, p. 294)

This leads us on to reflect on the link between interaction and the social and affective aspect of language learning.

Social Importance of Interaction for Children and Adolescents

As reflected in the comment by the high school student learning French, another vital aspect of interaction in the L2 classroom and one that is important for learning relates to the importance of social interactions for children and adolescents. Dunn (1999), an educational researcher talking about language between children notes, 'What is common across so many child-child interactions—and especially those between friends—is that they matter to the children; their emotional salience is unquestionable' (p. 270).

In the foreign language classroom, because the majority language is the L1 and most interactions outside the language classroom are carried out in the L1, it is these conversations that are likely to matter most to them. However, in the L2 context, where the language of the classroom is also the language of the community, social positioning and friendships are negotiated and develop through interaction in the target language. In this case, the target language is a vehicle through which relationships are established, defined, and worked out. A number of studies among younger and older learners in schools have highlighted both the positive and negative sides to the social nature of interaction between peers. In Classroom Snapshot 1.2, we saw an example of this where three kindergarten children, while constructing with bricks, excitedly talk about their work together. For the language learner, Y, this provides a positive experience with her peers, and helps her to participate in the interaction with them as an equal despite her limited language. Through this she both connects with her peers socially and emotionally, and gains important linguistic input.

In contrast, research also shows how native-speaker peers can act as gatekeepers to opportunities for using the target language. For example, Toohey (1998), describing L2 interaction in elementary (K-3) classrooms in

Canada, and Barnard (2009), an upper primary classroom (year 5) in New Zealand, both found differential success among the learners. Their finding, that some second language learners were more successful than others was attributed to a number of factors, including the teacher's perception of the child and the teacher's classroom practices such as separating the L2 learners from the other learners in the class. Such research suggests that when children are isolated from working with more capable peers they miss out on their company as a resource for learning. They also become further removed from the goal of being able to participate as members of the classroom community.

In a longitudinal study of ten adolescent students newly arrived in Australia, Miller (2000; 2003) found that only some students made friends among their native-speaker peers. Many were marginalized and socially isolated from the Australian born students. Miller reflects on the learners' renegotiation of social identities within these new settings. She emphasizes that while students had limited control in this process, personal characteristics such as willingness to communicate, resilience, and an outgoing personality made a difference. As Miller reports:

> *For those students who were marginalised, high schools were ... places where you were physically and socially isolated within the ESL unit; realised you didn't speak properly; had to catch up with the others; felt lost; didn't understand the tests, the texts, or the assemblies; and had to rely on L1 friends for all social interaction.*

(Miller, 2003, p. 181)

Longitudinal research in schools, such as that carried out by Toohey and by Miller, provides an important reminder for us to pay attention to the social consequence of interaction in the school context. In the classroom, the teacher can play a role in fostering positive relationships between students. Encouraging collaboration between learners, building up positive experiences between students who are not alike can be a way of breaking down barriers. Other work suggests strategies for fostering collaborative interaction and strengthening relationships between peers. For example, Dörnyei & Murphey (2003) emphasize how important it is to take the time to foster group cohesion and create positive classroom environments in the class as a whole, as well as pair- and group-work.

Formulaic Language

It is helpful to recognize that another aspect of peer interaction in classrooms concerns the use of formulaic language. Whether we are native speakers, advanced language learners, or beginners, much of our language is formulaic. Think about common phrases such as 'How are you?', 'What do you want to do tonight?', 'Did you have a good weekend?' (famously presented as 'djavagudweekend?' in an Australian advertisement for insect repellant). These strings of words come quickly because we say them so often. We depend on formulaic language to help us speak fluently, and doing so reduces the burden in processing language for speech. Further, our interlocutors find it easier and more efficient to understand us because of our use of predictable sequences. Wray (2002) describes such formulaic sequences as a prefabricated sequence of words, meaning that it is stored and retrieved whole from memory—it is not created by the learners themselves, serving as a kind of database of language from which learners can draw.

In the classroom, such chunks of language also provide the learner with a means of participation even when their proficiency is very low. When the teacher follows a predictable routine, with familiar language, learners are able to guess what they should say or do. In primary schools this can include songs, rhymes, and familiar stories. In secondary schools, this might include formal greetings, particular phrases used in the classroom such as 'May I leave the room?', 'Excuse me, what does this mean?', and even more complex academic language, such as 'I dis/agree because ... '. Eventually, these chunks become worked out as parts, and used in productive ways. For example, in a study of high school learners of French in England, Myles, Mitchell, & Hooper (1999) found that the students built up a repertoire of rote-learned questions, from which they were gradually able to generate a wide range of questions in French by substituting different vocabulary items.

Social Goals

Formulaic language also contributes to children's social goals. When they use the language of their peers, they reinforce ties of affiliation. For example, Wong Fillmore (1976), in a year-long study of five Spanish-speaking children in an ESL setting, notes a reliance on formulas and single words in the peer interaction between each child and an English-speaking classmate. Wong Fillmore emphasizes the importance of peer interaction as a key context for input and L2 use specifically because it offers the language of peers. As she notes, 'children ... acquire expressions in the context of social situations *which are important to them*, figure out patterns on the basis of these expressions they know how to use and pick up vocabulary items by freeing them from formulaic expressions' (1979, pp. 728–9, our emphasis).

Their productive use of formulaic expressions stems from the social and emotional importance it holds for them.

Spotlight Study 2.3

A study by Philp & Duchesne (2008) examined the contribution of peers to the language learning of one young child in a kindergarten class. Yessara was a six-year-old child with very minimal English when she arrived at a rural primary school in Australia. Over six weeks, following her first month of school, the researchers recorded Yessara's interactions with her peers and with the teachers, both before school and during classroom group activities.

They transcribed and analyzed seven recordings. They found that peers seldom provided scaffolding or feedback to the extent that the teacher did, and that the language they used with Yessara was highly variable—sometimes quite complex, but sometimes like baby talk such as 'me go up canteen … you come with me and me buy some frogs for you' (p. 93).

In the following example, Yessara sits drawing at a table with two classmates, Emily and Elsa, before school starts. When her friend Roberta arrives, Yessara bursts forth excitedly to gain her attention, using the very phrase Emily had used earlier (line 3), 'very colorful zebra', and Yessara succeeds in becoming the focus of conversation. It is interesting in this example that the pattern of interaction seen in lines 1, 4 and 5 (Q: 'What's this?' A: 'animal') is repeated again in the conversation between Yessara and Roberta. The predictable and repetitive nature of much of classroom discourse can be an asset to the new language learner.

1	**Emily:**	That's blu:e. What's this? Zebra?
2	**Yessara:**	Yeah.
3	**Emily:**	Very colorful zebra. [baby talk lilting intonation]
4	**Emily:**	What's that?
5	**Elsa:**	The elephant

[several turns later]

6	**Emily:**	[Roberta arrives] Oh hello Roberta I thought you were sick.
7	**Roberta:**	No mum XX.
8	**Yessara:**	[excitedly] Look at the zebra very colorful zebra isn't it? Very very colorful.
9	**Roberta:**	What's this?
10	**Yessara:**	Tiger. [laughing]
11	**Emily:**	I'll eat you. [sing-song voice]
12	**Yessara:**	Ele:phant.
13	**Emily:**	Yeah elephant.

(Philp & Duchesne, 2008, p. 94, unpublished extension: lines 9–13)

Philp & Duchesne argue that children's peer interaction can provide important learning opportunities for young second language learners in mainstream classrooms that are quite different to those provided by interaction with the teacher. In this example, as they note 'other children's speech can provide chunks which then scaffold Yessara's own production' (p. 94). The authors go on to argue that such interaction is also shaped by and, in turn, fulfills particular social goals of developing friendships and taking her place in the class as an equal with others. Using the language of peers not only helps her language development, but also strengthens friendships with peers, which in turn helps her build her social and communicative competence. ▨

This study echoes the findings of many studies among children in the early primary years: children can adopt the language of the peers to align themselves with one another, and this can contribute to their success in L2 learning. For example, in a study of four Japanese preschoolers in a bilingual program, Perera interprets children's appropriation of language from teachers and peers in the classroom as allowing them to become 'not only linguistically, but also socially, connected to the community in which the language is used' (2001, p. 11). Peer acceptance is vital, given its key role in L2 learning, as a context for input and L2 use. Wray underscores this when she notes: 'In children of primary school age, the degree of success in L2 learning seems to depend in part on their social alliances with peers' (2002, p. 148).

Promoting positive relationships between peers can be critical to success in language learning in the second language context. Even in foreign language classrooms, working alongside friends, feeling relaxed, and having fun trying out the new language regardless of mistakes is a positive environment for learning. This social side to interaction should not be forgotten! At the same time, from what we have outlined in the first part of this chapter, it is clear that as teachers we must also be aware of the cognitive processes.

Individual Differences

So far in this chapter, we have generalized about the nature and outcomes of oral interaction for second language learners in classrooms, but as we know, every child is different. Any teacher can fondly (and not so fondly) recount stories of uniqueness—the students who are always first to speak up, others who prefer to work independently; the risk-takers who will try anything and don't worry about mistakes, versus those who play it safe. Some students love language learning and work hard at it; others have no interest at all. There are the individuals who seem particularly gifted—they easily memorize vocabulary, perfectly mimic accents, or seem naturally able to notice patterns in language. Others struggle to perceive or remember words, pronunciation, or grammatical patterns.

Researchers (for example, Dörnyei, 2006; Ellis, 2004, 2008; Skehan, 1986, 1998) generally agree that individual differences do have an effect on learning. Ellis (2008), for example, describes how cognitive 'abilities' such as memory, aptitude, and 'propensities' such as learning style, motivation, personality types (for example, extroversion, openness to new experiences), anxiety, and willingness to communicate will impact upon language learning success. Based on your own experience as a language learner or teacher, what individual abilities and propensities would you expect to be particularly important to successful language learning? If you were to pick just two factors as being most important to language learning, what would they be?

Individual difference research has predominantly been conducted among adult learners, and in reference to second language learning in general, but there have been some studies of younger learners that are relevant to the question of how individual differences might impact the potential effectiveness of oral interaction for language learning in primary and secondary schools. We explore some of this research below and again in Chapters 3 and 4 in relation to younger and older school-aged learners.

Learning Style and Personality Traits

In both primary and secondary schools, educators recognize that learners range greatly in learning styles and personality, and that their predispositions or preferences for ways of learning are not always catered for. Studies of oral language among child learners show that gregariousness, talkativeness, and responsiveness are all traits that help successful learners maintain conversation with others (for example, Strong, 1983; Wong Fillmore, 1979). Similarly, studies with older learners suggest that extraversion gives learners an advantage in oral tasks (Dewaele & Furnham, 1999). For example, in a study of Dutch teenagers (aged 11–13 years), Verhoeven & Vermeer (2002) found that certain personality traits, particularly openness to experience, predicted learners' communicative competence.

These studies suggest that certain traits or propensities can assist language learners, and give them an advantage on particular types of tasks. However, it is not so straightforward as to say that strength in a particular trait guarantees success in language learning. Rather, there is a complex dynamic between the many characteristics of any person and the learning context. It is a composite of these that may contribute to success in language learning.

At present, researchers tend to think that motivation and aptitude are the two individual difference factors that make the most difference to language learning. The role of motivation and aptitude are not the whole story though. It is also important to note that the purpose and context of learning makes a difference in how these factors affect learning. In the following section we will look at each one in turn: first, for what research in general says about why they are important, and then in relation to research about these with children and adolescents and the implications this may have for teaching.

Aptitude

Working memory

When we talk about **aptitude**, we are not talking about a single ability—we are really referring to a group of interrelated cognitive abilities, all of which seem to underlie our facility to learn new languages. Cognitive psychologists, Miyake & Friedman (1998), argued that **working memory** could be the most important aspect of aptitude. In fact, in a study among Hungarian high school students, Sáfár & Kormos (2008) found students' working memory was a better prediction of success in intensive English classes than general aptitude. Working memory is the ability to store and process relevant bits of information all at the same time (for example, Field, 2003; Harrington & Sawyer, 1992). When we try to work out the best deal at a supermarket by calculating in our heads the cost of ten single apples versus a bag of ten apples, we use our working memory—we 'store' (retain) in our heads the cost of both items, and we calculate (process) the sum mentally. Similarly, when we talk with others we use our working memory as we store and simultaneously process what people say, and as we respond to it. In our first language this is automatic, but we can find it difficult if the conversation is fast and the content is complex or novel. As we noted earlier, second language learners encounter even greater difficulty because so much is not automatic—too much information needs to be retained and processed all at once.

While we all have the working memory we need for everyday situations, people can differ in their ability to store and process information simultaneously, and some may have particularly 'high' or 'low' working memory. The advantages of high working memory are most likely to be seen when the demands of a task are complex (for example, in a conversation with many participants, or with a lot of new, difficult, or interrelated content). The learning context itself plays a big part in how useful those abilities are. As Robinson (2005) suggests 'some learners … may be especially suited to learning under one condition, from one technique, or on one task versus others.' (p. 2.) However, other researchers suggest that teachers can 'level the playing field' (for example, Erlam, 2005; Sáfár & Kormos, 2008): some teaching methods may compensate for differences in working memory and other aspects of aptitude.

For example, in a study among Japanese 5th-Graders (primary school learners), Ando et al. (1992) compared two groups of learners who experienced different types of instruction: 20 hours of either explicit form-focused instruction or more implicit communicatively-oriented instruction (including meaning-focused production activities). In the explicit form-focused class, it was the learners with high working memory who were more successful. This type of instruction seemed to favor these learners. However, it was the learners with low working memory who were more successful in the communicatively oriented class. This study suggests that, with regard to working memory ability and language learning, different types of instruction can suit different types of people. This supports current practices that advocate flexibility in teaching, including a combination of approaches. We will discuss this further in Chapter 4 as we think about learning at different ages.

Language analytic ability

Another aspect of aptitude is what Skehan (1998) calls 'language analytic ability'. Some learners are better than others at thinking abstractly about language or noticing patterns in language, an ability that matures in adolescence, but is already developing in the late primary years. With varying degrees of success, adolescents are able to make generalizations about language and infer rules or recognize that words have similar grammatical functions (for example, recognize the noun in a sentence), just from hearing or reading examples of language use. With regard to language analytic ability, the research also suggests that the importance of aptitude for success depends on the type of instruction. Some research in secondary school settings and among students in the late primary years (for example, Erlam, 2005; Ranta, 2002; White, 2008) suggests that structured teaching approaches, where patterns in language are explicitly pointed out, can help those learners who do not naturally find it easy to work it out for themselves. We will look at these studies in Chapters 3 and 4.

Motivation

When it comes to instructed language learning, aptitude alone doesn't guarantee success. **Motivation** also plays an important role. Dörnyei (2001a, p. 8) provides a straightforward definition for us:

Motivation is responsible for:
- Why people decide to do something
- How long they are willing to sustain the activity
- How hard they are going to pursue it.

Children don't often have much choice about language learning, it is often just part of the curriculum. This is less the case for adolescents. Interestingly, within school settings, what motivates children to try hard and to keep on with a language can change with age, as we will see in later chapters.

Summary

In this chapter, we have emphasized the various ways in which interaction promotes language learning. As teachers, it is important to be aware of the cognitive and social processes that appear to contribute to language learning, and then to create opportunities and situations that foster and support these. Through talking with others, learners are helped to make sense of second language input, slightly beyond the language they have already acquired. In struggling to understand and to be understood, learners are pushed in their language output. Language is repeated, reformulated, and negotiated in ways that highlight the relationship between form and meaning. This and other types of feedback can draw learners' attention to language difficulties and ways to resolve them. Continual practice in language use is essential, too, for assisting learners in moving from declarative to procedural knowledge and promoting fluency. In part because of the emotional salience of the language of peers and the social nature of interaction, social, and linguistic goals often go hand in hand. Thus, promoting positive relationships between peers can be critical to success in language learning in the second language context. Even in foreign language classrooms, working alongside friends, feeling relaxed, and having fun trying out the new language regardless of mistakes creates a positive environment for learning, and can be motivating for learning. It is important not to lose sight of the social aspects to interaction.

3 Oral Interaction in the Primary Classroom Context: Research and Implications for Pedagogy

Preview

In exploring the importance of oral interaction for language learning, we have seen that learners are active participants in the process of interaction. A special focus of Chapter 2 was how interaction promotes those aspects of speaking and listening that facilitate language learning. This included a discussion of input and output, practice, and automaticity. We noted how interaction allows learners to give and to receive feedback on language, and we showed how this helps learners to notice problems in their own production. We also considered how interaction leads learners to engage with their new language, and with each other, highlighting the social aspect of language learning.

As part of our discussion we have commented on the impact of the context of the language learning and of learners' characteristics. Language learning will look different in second language and foreign language classrooms, in content and immersion situations. It will also differ according to such things as the age of the learners.

In this chapter, we will examine how younger children interact with each other and with their teachers, in different classroom contexts. We will also look at how their unique characteristics influence this interaction that, in turn, may present pedagogical advantages, but also challenges. We are especially interested in answering the following questions:

- How does interaction contribute to learning language in the primary school context?
- What are the implications of this for our teaching practice?

Child Second Language Learners

The importance of age to language learning will not come as any surprise to those working in schools. Teachers, parents, and anyone with experience working with younger people are all too aware of how different the interactions of younger children are from those of older children, and how these differ again from the type of interaction that occurs with adolescents. In addition, the way that teachers talk to children is vastly different from the ways they interact with older learners (Oliver, 1997).

Look at Classroom Snapshots 3.1 and 3.2. Which do you think happened in a language classroom for children, and which in an adult classroom?

Classroom Snapshot 3.1

1 **Teacher:**   Now does anyone have any other information about those two pieces of news? The first piece was about the police who have caught two people who they think set fire to the French embassy. And the second piece of news was about the shop that collapsed in um Korea and many people have died. Does anyone have any other information?

2 **Student 1:** Nup.

3 **Student 2:** Nope.

4 **Teacher:**   No has anyone got any questions they want to ask?

5 **Student 3:** No.

6 **Student 4:** Ah.

7 **Student 5:** Maybe it's silly question. How did they caught them= did= when the police came and then= did they ran away or did they just stopped?

8 **Student 4:** Oh they had they had a video camera on the Embassy and they and they saw a car a white car coming they ah they photed the registrate registrate number and then they= then they sent that to police and then police find [vere] they live.

Classroom Snapshot 3.2

1 **Teacher:** What can we see in this picture? What can you see here? Is it part of an animal?

2 **Students:** No it's a jungle.

3 **Teacher:** It's a jungle because you've read the word jungle. It's jungle. What's a jungle? Joseph?

4 **J:**   It's on the XX.

5 **Teacher:** Animals live in a jungle?

6 **J:**   Some.

7 **Teacher:** Some. Good word. Some animals live in a jungle. So what is a jungle? What is in a jungle?

8 **Students:** It's like a forest.

  9 **Teacher:**   It's like a forest. That's right.
 10 **Students:** It's like woods.
 11 **Teacher:**   It's like woods. It's full of trees big trees in the jungle where
                animals can hide and can live. Now the next picture have got no
                water and it's got a hot hot sun. I wonder what sort of place that
                is? XX?

(Oliver, Philp, & Mackey, unpublished data) ▨

From the style of classroom interaction and the topic of their discussions, it is quite apparent that the second snapshot occurred with younger learners and the first with adults. In this chapter we will closely examine interaction between and with children aged approximately 5–12 years. Although this covers less than a decade, it is a considerable time span in the life of a child.

Child Development

When children begin school they are still in a period described as 'early childhood'. After the first two to three years of school, they move into a phase called 'middle childhood'. Before they move on to their secondary education, some will be well on their way to adolescence. During this time they will change considerably: their thought processes will dramatically alter, as will the way in which they socialize and the types of relationships they have with others—all of which is reflected in the language they use and the way they interact (Berk, 2013; Duchesne et al., 2013). An example of this is that when a child is at the age to start school, although still egocentric in nature, they are beginning to take account of other people's perspectives and this is reflected in their language and language skills, such as an improved ability to take turns and to stay 'on-topic' (even when it is not one they initiated). This is quite different from very young preschool children who are less able to take turns and who switch quickly from one topic to another. For the purposes of this book we have grouped all the primary-aged students together as it is difficult in a book of this scope to do otherwise. Be aware, however, that aspects we cover will differ according to the age and stage of development of the learner across the primary school years.

In terms of oral interaction research, fewer studies have been done with primary school learners than with older language learners. So in this chapter we will draw on the comparatively small body of research that has explored oral interaction for this age group, highlighting three projects in particular in our Spotlight Studies. It should be noted that of the research that has been done, more is experimental, rather than classroom-based. Although the number of published primary school classroom studies is growing, there is by no means a substantial body of work. As a consequence much of what we do as primary school teachers in terms of supporting second language development through oral interaction is based upon intuition or a modification of principles designed for older learners, including adults. We hope that this chapter will go some way to addressing this shortcoming.

Age and Second Language Acquisition

We know that age makes a difference in language learning, and in different ways according to various contextual factors. For instance, in second language contexts involving living in, being educated in, and then working in the target language over a long period of time (such as immigrant children in ESL contexts in Australia, Canada, and the USA), younger children seem to be advantaged in terms of language learning outcomes. Therefore, one potential advantage for primary school students in mainstream settings is associated with their **ultimate attainment** of **native like ability**. If you are familiar with the fable of 'The Tortoise and the Hare', then the analogy would be that children are the tortoises: they start slowly, but eventually will 'win' at second language learning. This is because it becomes increasingly more difficult to achieve native-like ability in a new language the older you are when you begin learning. This is particularly the case with phonology. Many older second language users acquire excellent grammar and vocabulary knowledge but still find it impossible to 'sound like' a person who began to learn the language in early childhood. Long describes this effect as **maturational constraints** (Long, 1990). Others have described the effects of age in different ways (Birdsong, 2005; Paradis, 2007).

However, this is not to say that younger is always better. Outcomes will depend on a number of factors including the quality of the learning environment, (for example, the nature and quantity of input provided) and type of language learning context. For example, where language input and time are limited, such as in foreign language classes (where children usually share a common first language and perhaps learn another language in just a few short lessons each week) older children, particularly adolescents, can have the advantage. Despite a long-held and common belief that second language learning is easier for children, there is considerable evidence that adults and adolescents initially do better because they have the cognitive, strategic, and social skills that enhance their language learning journey (Burstall, 1975; Muñoz, 2006; Snow & Hoefnagel-Hohle, 1978). They are able to use their superior memory, metalinguistic knowledge, and analytic skills to help them, as we shall discuss in Chapter 4.

Language Learning in Different Settings

As we saw in Chapter 2, regardless of whether the learners are adults or children, interaction serves a vital role in assisting the development that does occur. This can occur in a variety of settings—at home (especially for bilingual learners), within the context of the extended family or community, and for many, at school. As we have just described, language learning may occur in foreign language classes—that is, where the target language is not the language of the wider community. For example, in English-speaking countries this would include the teaching of languages other than English, such as Japanese, French, Italian, and Mandarin. Such teaching may include formal instruction, where the language is treated as another curriculum subject area, and in primary school is typically very limited in time (for example, 30–90 minutes per week) (Tognini & Oliver, 2012), and restricted in the opportunity for individual oral production. On the other hand, the learning of a foreign language may occur in foreign-language immersion classrooms so that students study different curriculum areas, such as social studies, science, or math through the medium of the target language. For example, children with an English-speaking background being taught math using French as the language of instruction (Lightbown, 2013; Lyster, 2007). Some children may also be learning a second language in environments where the language being taught is that spoken by many within the community and where it is the main language used in the classroom. Such learning can occur within the mainstream classroom—as often happens in schools where there is a high proportion of children of migrant parents living nearby. Alternatively, such programs may be taught in intensive classes for newly arrived students.

Therefore, there is a wide range of language learning that may be distinguished by:

1 the amount of time—ranging from quite limited to quite extensive, such as in the immersion context
2 the opportunities for input and production—again these can be limited to instruction mostly in the students L1, to all communication undertaken in the target language
3 the approach taken—for instance, from Communicative Language Teaching which remains influential in many ESL classrooms through to Task-Based Language Teaching which is being used by more teachers of

children (Oliver & Bogachenko, to appear). More traditional methods also continue in foreign language settings, whilst Content-Based Language Teaching (Lightbown, 2013) is common in immersion and ESL contexts.

Context of Learning

The context of the learning, for example, whether it occurs during formal instruction inside a classroom or informally in social situations, will have an impact on how interaction occurs and the opportunities it affords the learners, particularly in terms of interaction (Alcón & García Mayo, 2009; García Mayo & Alcón, 2002). For example, outside the classroom, Tarone & Liu (1995) found that a five-year-old called Bob produced utterances of different complexity according to whom he was interacting with and according to the topic of discussion. Recently Lyster & Ranta (2013) highlight the differences in interactions that occur inside the classroom, particularly in relation to the type of feedback that is provided. Similarly, Oliver & Mackey (2003) demonstrated that, according to the teacher's focus, context made a difference to interaction, including feedback, even within lessons (see Chapter 2).

Now consider Classroom Snapshots 3.3 and 3.4. Look at how the teacher provides feedback in Classroom Snapshot 3.3 by way of a clarification request, but does not provide any feedback in Classroom Snapshot 3.4. Why do you think this might be?

Classroom Snapshot 3.3

The class members are playing a game, taking turns to describe animals for others to guess what the animal might be.

1 **Student:**   Who has fin?
2 **Teacher:**   Sorry I beg your pardon?
3 **Student:**   Who has fin[s]?

(Oliver & Mackey, 2003, p. 519)

Classroom Snapshot 3.4

The teacher is previewing a text before the class reads the story.

1 **Teacher:**   OK now you tell us all about that what that part= part of the picture is about. Look at the book.
2 **Student:**   When um Little Red Riding Hood when she at river XX she saw someone in the woodshed she went deeper deeper in the wood

forward and then he he ran first into the house XX the wolf ran
first and then Little Riding Hood got first and then he'll knock on
the door and Little Riding Hood will know the wolf is there.

3 **Teacher:**   Good. OK. Sit down. That's right.

(Oliver & Mackey, unpublished data) ▨

It would appear that in Classroom Snapshot 3.3 the teacher is concerned with understanding the student, focusing her attention on the communicative intent within the exchange. Thus she poses a question for clarification. This in turn results in modified output by that student. In contrast, in Classroom Snapshot 3.4, the teacher appears to be focused on progressing through the reading lesson, and sharing meaning about the class reading book is her central focus. As a consequence, when a student's contribution is not target-like, the teacher ignores this and moves on with the lesson.

Context and Types of Feedback

The language context of the classroom appears to impact not only on the provision, but also on the uptake of feedback. For example, Lyster & Mori (2006) found differences in how students responded to **prompts** and recasts in Japanese and French immersion classes, 'with the largest proportion of repair resulting from prompts in French immersion and from recasts in Japanese immersion' (p. 269). The research described in Spotlight Study 3.1 was undertaken in primary school classrooms. In this study, differences in the uptake of feedback by students were also found, but this time dependent not on the lesson context, but rather on the nature of the recasts provided.

Spotlight Study 3.1

Oliver & Grote (2010) observed child ESL learners who had been learning English for less than a year. They compared the provision and use of recasts as corrective feedback in children's interactions with different people. They recorded the ESL children's interactions as they talked, either with a teacher (T–NNS) in a classroom, in a pairwork setting with another ESL learner (NNS–NNS), or with a peer of an English-speaking background (NNS–NS).

For the first type of interactions (T–NNS), five teachers were recorded working with their small classes (10–16 students) of primary school-aged ESL learners. In the second and third groups, there were 12 NNS–NNS and 12 NNS–NS pairs of children, aged 10–13 years, working together. Using the taxonomy of recasts (see Table 3.1) developed by Sheen (2006) for research with adults in a classroom context, the researchers compared the provision, opportunity for use, and actual use of recasts in the interactions in the three contexts.

Category	Description
Multi move recasts	
Corrective	Recasts include a repetition of the error, but with correction
Repeated	Recasts are repeated partially or fully
Combination	Recasts include other types of feedback, such as metalinguistic information (e.g. in response to 'I used transportations', the interlocutor says, '"Transport" uncountable')
Single change recasts	
Mode	As declaratives or interrogatives
Scope	Isolated (on their own) or incorporated into a fuller utterance
Reduction	Reduced from original form or not reduced
Length	Word/short phrase, clause, or longer phrase
Number of changes	One or multiple changes to the original utterance
Type of change	Addition, deletion, substitution, reordering, or combination
Linguistic focus	Pronunciation, vocabulary, or grammar

Table 3.1 Taxonomy of recasts (adapted from Sheen, 2006)

There were 84 recasts in the teacher-fronted classes, 58 in the NNS–NNS pairs and 74 in the NNS–NS dyads. Like Sheen (2006), Oliver & Grote (2010) found that only a few recasts were given in ways that involved multiple changes:

1 **NNS:**   What is far?
2 **NS:**   Like how far apart? Like that far apart or that far apart? How far apart are they?
3 **NNS:**   Yeah.

(Oliver & Grote, 2010, p. 26.8)

The majority of the recasts were single change recasts, like that in the following example:

1 **NNS:**   The two brothers went inside and slum=
2 **Teacher:** =Slammed.
3 **NNS:**   Slammed the door.

(Oliver & Grote, unpublished data)

However, the way that some recasts in different categories were provided to children varied not only from the findings with adults of Sheen (2006) but also across the three child contexts. A summary of how these recasts differed is shown in Table 3.2. The first column indicates the specific feature of a single recast move; the second indicates how this specific single recast move differed across the T–NNS, NNS–NNS and NS–NNS pairs of children and the third column indicates how these child comparisons that are reported in Oliver & Grote (2010) differ from the adults reported in Sheen (2006).

Characteristic of single recast move	Comparison between the three child context results	Comparison of child (Oliver & Grote, 2010) and adult (Sheen, 2006) results
Mode	Different More declaratives in classroom context More interrogatives in pair-work context	Classroom results similar Pair-work results different
Scope	Similar	Different Higher proportion in child context
Reduction	Different Higher proportion in NNS–NS pair-work and least in classroom context	Different Higher proportion of reduction in adult context
Length	Different Higher proportion of shorter length recasts in pair-work context	Similar for NNS–NS context and adult classroom Different for NNS–NNS and T–NNS contexts and adult classroom
Number of changes	Similar	Different Higher proportion of only one change in adult context
Type of change	Similar	Different Higher proportion of substitution recasts in adult context
Linguistic focus	Similar	Similar

Table 3.2 Summary of recast findings (adapted from Oliver & Grote, 2010, p. 26.20)

Despite some of the apparent differences in the findings across the three contexts, it was found that children working in pairs were able to provide the same type of feedback to that of the teachers, although overall the uptake by children was less than that of adults.

Sheen's study with adults did not examine the opportunity for learners to use the feedback they received in the form of recasts. However, Oliver & Grote did examine it and found that the least opportunity occurred for learners interacting with teachers. Students had 'no chance' to use the feedback in 61% of the instances after a recast was provided (for example, because of a topic switch, the teacher moving on to ask another question, or talking to another student). In comparison, there was greater opportunity, particularly in the NNS–NNS context (i.e. when learners worked together in pairs). Overall, Oliver & Grote concluded that:

> *it is just not sufficient to examine the provision and use of feedback from a cognitive perspective, the environment and the characteristics of the learners and the context in which they are interacting, that is the social contributions to interaction, also need to be considered.*
>
> (Oliver & Grote, 2010, p. 26.20) ▪

For teachers, the findings of Spotlight Study 3.1 highlight the role that peers can play, not only in providing useful feedback, but also doing so in a situation that is potentially more conducive to uptake than in a teacher-fronted classroom. We will return to this issue later in this chapter. What studies such as this also suggest is that context is an important factor to consider with respect to different aspects of interaction. Therefore, in this book we have attempted to provide examples taken from a variety of contexts, including ESL, EFL and foreign language learning.

Contribution of Teacher–Student Interaction

When young children start school there are many things they must adjust to in order to learn successfully. For example, they need to get used to a new environment outside their home, to being surrounded by more peers, and to a range of different adults, as well as to interacting in new ways with all these people. These adjustments may be challenging for some individuals, for instance, if their level of maturity makes it difficult for them to function successfully away from their family. It may also be more challenging if they lack a familiarity with school environments—this is especially the case for the oldest sibling in an immigrant family. For others, their level of physical development or their personalities may inhibit a successful transition into school. Beginning school may be particularly challenging for those who do not have the language used in school as their first language. The circumstances of the child may also make the task of transitioning into the classroom more difficult. Consider, for example, the experience of a child who is a refugee with no previous experience of schooling, and who may have never previously seen a school. Going to school for the first time may be far more difficult for this child compared to a child who has attended kindergarten or pre-school. Consider how much more difficult again this would be if the child arrives as a refugee, not at the age when most children start school, but instead at the age of 11 or 12 years.

Activity 3.1

Look at these case studies based on real children we have taught during our years as ESL teachers. Outline the challenges you think they may face as they begin school, especially the challenge of learning a new language at school.

Case study 1

An 11-year-old Cambodian child arrives at school for the first time accompanied by his grandmother. His parents and siblings are all dead. Despite spending the majority of his life in a refugee camp, he has never attended school before and is illiterate in his first language, Khmer. He does not speak a word of English.

Case study 2

An 8-year-old Sudanese girl arrives at school. She has several other younger and older siblings, but she is the oldest girl. Her mother is a single parent as her father went missing during the war in her homeland. She has had some very traditional English lessons on an irregular basis in the refugee camp where she lived for three years. She writes some English words and has some literacy in her first language.

Case study 3

A 6-year-old Japanese boy has accompanied his parents and older brother to Australia. They are 'business migrants' and are well educated. They have very high expectations for him. He attended kindergarten in Japan, but has no English at all.

Learning to Interact in New Ways

As they enter school, all children need to adapt to new and different environments than they are used to being in, but the challenge will vary amongst different individuals. As teachers, we need to be aware of the challenges children confront as they begin school and provide the type of support to enable them to transition successfully into their education journey.

In terms of language, one challenge for many younger children concerns the formality of the classroom. Although contemporary Early Childhood education promotes learning through play—a less formal approach to learning than traditionally existed (Fasoli & Johns, 2007; Malaguzzi, 1996)—younger learners must still learn a new set of rules for the way to behave in a context more formal than their previous experience. They also need to learn new ways of interacting and to adjust to the different opportunities to do so. For example, they move from being in situations such as the home or childcare setting, where the adult to child ratio is higher and where there are few others with whom they have to share the attention of their parents/carers, to the classroom where many other children need attention. This means that at school the opportunity to interact with an adult may be diminished. Therefore, for all children regardless of home language background, as they enter formal learning in classrooms, the nature of their interactions, especially with adults, will change.

Teacher Talk

Teachers obviously have an important role to play, not only in children's learning generally, but also because of their potential to contribute to a child's language development and to their ability to interact appropriately in a variety of contexts. Yet despite recognizing this vital role and a long-standing recognition of the place of talk in learning and for learning (Barnes, 1976; Britton, 1970), the type of interaction that is most prominent in many classrooms is the teacher doing most of the talking, and addressing the class as a whole (i.e. one-to-many). This contrasts to the situation in the home where children often interact with adults one-to-one or few-to-one, such as when they are talking to a parent with their siblings. Outside the classroom, children are often in a position to initiate the talk, and depending on the adult(s) with whom they are conversing, do a lot of the talking. This is quite unlike the situation that occurs in many classrooms. In fact, Edwards & Mercer (1994) describe classroom interaction as abiding by the two-thirds rule, namely two-thirds of the talk is the teacher's and two thirds of this teacher talk consists of asking questions and lecturing. As such, compared to the home environment, there is less opportunity for students to interact and to talk-to-learn, especially as part of one-to-one interactions with an adult.

Patterns of Interaction

When a teacher does talk to an individual in the classroom, the pattern of interaction may follow the more formal 'initiate-respond-evaluate' cycle, sometimes also referred to as an **IRF pattern** and described some time ago by Mehan (1979) and then Cazden (2001). This also means that when a teacher interacts with an individual student in a one-to-one situation, all others in the class are effectively excluded from the talk until the teacher indicates that it is their turn. In classrooms where teachers feel increasingly under pressure to cover the curriculum, reach prescribed standards (McKay, 2005), and prepare students for such things as national testing, many students may not get their turn to speak. In fact, it has been found that teachers ask easier or no questions at all of those students who enter schooling without the language of the classroom (for example, ESL students in Australia, Canada, or the USA) (Ho, 2005). Effectively, this means that those who are in need of the most practice at using their new language are typically the ones that get the least opportunity to do so. This is something we need to be very conscious of and work hard to overcome. To counter the lack of opportunity to interact in class and to facilitate peer learning, especially for those students learning a second language, many teachers incorporate opportunities for group-work into their daily teaching practice. We will discuss group-work and peer interaction later in the chapter.

Teacher Modifications

Whilst what we have outlined above suggests some negative aspects to classroom teacher talk, there is a long history of research and (of particular relevance to this book) of research in second language classrooms, that investigates how teachers modify their language in ways that do support their students. For example, teachers have been found to vary their vocabulary according to the extent of their students' lexical knowledge (Wong Fillmore, 1985) and the rate of their speech depending on the proficiency level of their students (Chaudron, 1988). Gibbons (2006) also provides numerous examples of the way that teachers use repetition, reformulation, and explanation to scaffold learners' understanding and to support their use of language appropriate to specific purposes, and to generate meaningful interactions. You can see in Classroom Snapshot 3.5 how the teacher helps the students to develop their understanding about working appropriately in groups. She does so by building upon the students' own contributions about how this is done, including repeating key words and phrases, asking questions, and keeping it in the 'here and now'.

Classroom Snapshot 3.5

Teacher–students whole class

1	**Teacher:**	… 'I know what we're doing me me me I've decided?' Is that how we work in groups?	Exaggerates student's own words
2	**Students:**	No.	
3	**Teacher:**	What sort of things can we remember Simon?	
4	**Student:**	Em share your ideas?	Repeats and rephrases
5	**Teacher:**	Good. Take turns. Share your ideas … Fabiola?	

6	**F:**	Communicate with your group.	
7	**Teacher:**	How do you communicate with your group … that's very true but how do you do it?	Elicits concrete examples
8	**F:**	Like instead of em when you start with your group you don't em shout … and don't 'I know what we should do and this is what I can do' and if someone want to talk it over say 'No this is what we're going to do.'	
9	**Teacher:**	OK so it's a lot of … first of all … turn-taking … and quiet group voices … and maybe sharing your ideas certainly 'Oh an idea I have' or 'One idea I have' or 'A suggestion that I have' … Put it forward as a suggestion … be careful … with the sort of group work language that you use. Well done.	Provides model of language

(Gibbons, 2006, pp. 191–92) ▨

Teachers can and do adapt the way they interact with the language learners in their classes. In some ways the type of modifications that they make parallels the way that parents interact with their very young children. For example, higher pitch and exaggerated intonation have been found to occur in **child-directed speech** (formerly called 'motherese') (Fernald & Simon, 1984) and in the language directed to language learners (Hatch, 1983), and seems to serve the same purpose in both places: to gain and maintain the language learner's attention and interest. There are a number of other things that teachers do and we ask you to reflect on these in Activity 3.2.

Activity 3.2
Consider the modifications that second language teachers have been found to make when interacting with their learners. Why might these be helpful? Are there any that could hinder language learning?

Area of language	Type of modification	How might this help or hinder language learning?
Phonological	• Rising intonation at the end of teacher utterances and not just for questions • Increased intelligibility and clear enunciation • Slower rate and more distinct pauses within and between utterances	Rising intonation invites agreement or disagreement and helps maintain attention
Syntactic	• Simpler utterances • Well-formed and grammatical utterances • More imperatives and questions, with declaratives increasing with the age of the learner	
Semantic	• More 'here and now' language, especially with younger learners • Less lexically diverse • More common and concrete words	
Pragmatic	• More questions • More direct than indirect requests • More self-repetition	

Photocopiable © Oxford University Press

Table 3.3 Reflection on teacher talk

It is clear that teachers may modify their language in various ways when talking to students, and these subtle changes support and encourage language learner development. Sometimes, however, modifications can actually hinder language learning, for example, through reducing opportunities for learners to hear complex speech, varied patterns of speech, or a wider range of vocabulary. Thus it is important to be conscious of the nature of the input being provided.

Demands of Classroom Talk

It is not just how teachers talk, it is also what they talk about that affects second language learners. Although the talk at school may be about personal things, as children continue their education the topics of conversation in the classroom become increasingly complex, more abstract, and further removed from their personal situation and the type of talk that occurs outside of school. Look at Classroom Snapshots 3.6 and 3.7—without labels it is clear which interaction occurred in a family or social situation and which one occurred in a classroom.

Classroom Snapshot 3.6

1 **Dima:**   [Another] piece of pizza the smaller than the other one.
2 **Sasha:**   And the uh something [good is].
3 **Dima:**   [Plea:se.]
4 **Sasha:**   That I rested XX [uh uh raced]=
5 **Dima:**   =[Yeaoooh.]
6 **John:**   Guys guys guys guys oh! Phw phw.
7 **Sasha:**   That I raced=
8 **John:**   =It's getting kind of loud.
9 **Sasha:**   =That I raced Inigo and I might nXX won. But I was the last one and Inigo! So I was jumping and I uh took another jump and almost there but I uh slipped and fell and I sprained my ankle.

(Fogle, 2008, p. 288)

Classroom Snapshot 3.7

1 **T:**   Something else that's very important … what else must you do? Philip? What else must you do … you also have to do something Belinda?
2 **B:**   You have to record what you did.
3 **T:**   You have to record … what you found … and what are we going to do tomorrow Philip?
4 **P:**   Em we're going to we're going to going to …
5 **T:**   What are we going to do tomorrow.
6 **P:**   We're going to tell … what we found out.
7 **T:**   Good boy. You were listening. That's good Philip … you're going to tell what you found out..

(Gibbons, 2006, p. 241) ■

Of course, the conversation in Classroom Snapshot 3.7 is from a classroom: the teacher checks to be sure these two second language learners have understood the homework instruction. It is also conceptually more challenging as it asks the learners to predict and to provide explanation. Classroom Snapshot 3.6 is an excerpt from dinnertime conversation between a father (John) and his two children, who are both second language speakers of English. You can see that their conversation involves a lot more overlapping of speech and the topics of conversation are vastly different from the academic discourse expected in schools.

However, not all language learning classroom contexts offer the opportunity for explorative interaction about cognitively demanding areas. For example, many students who spend eight or more years learning a foreign language are never able to do more than use greetings, ask or respond to simple questions, or follow simple directions (Tognini, 2008). The reasons for this are many and varied, including need, amount of input, practice and opportunity for use—all issues we covered in Chapter 1. Further, when students do begin learning a language, their linguistic proficiency may be such that for some period of time they may be restricted in their interactions—not only in what they can say, but also in terms of their understanding. In Spotlight Study 3.2, we can see how meaning remains unclear or opaque for language learners. At the same time, language learners may feel a sense of frustration because although they can undertake quite complex tasks in their first language, they are restricted to very basic interactions in their new language.

Spotlight Study 3.2

Ernst-Slavit & Mason (2011) undertook an in-depth study of the classroom talk of five teachers, examining in particular the oral academic language that they used. Ethnographic and sociolinguistic research methodologies were used. This included individual interviews with the teachers, classroom observations, video- and audio-taped recordings of the classroom, photographs, and the taking of field notes. The recordings were a particular focus of analysis with segments transcribed and analyzed to examine the absence or presence of the specialized and academic oral language of the classroom.

The findings showed that the teachers actually used a great deal of non-academic language during their lessons. For example, in one teacher's class she was found to use academic language in only ten percent of her interactions. Ernst-Slavit & Mason suggest that this reduces the opportunities for learners who do not come to school with the same 'linguistic capital' to learn the type of language that will assist them to acquire the academic discourse necessary for scholarly success.

In addition, and despite the fact that all the teachers had received ESL pedagogy preparation as part of their training, the language that they did use was at times less than clear and could 'possibly hinder understanding' (Ernst-Slavit & Mason, p. 433), especially for English language learning (ELL) students. For instance, some of the vocabulary they used involved homophones (words that sound the same but mean different things, for example, 'hair' and 'hare') and sometimes the words were heteronyms (words that are spelled the same but are pronounced differently and mean different things, for example, 'bow' = knot with two loose ends; front part of a boat or ship). Other times they used language such as deixis (for example, 'It's over there'), demonstratives (for example, 'this', 'those', 'him' and 'her') and idiomatic expressions. Ernst-Slavit & Mason give the example of the term 'that' used by one of the teachers: In the nine utterances she produces in a short exchange with her class, she uses the word 'that' five times and in each instance as a referent with a completely different meaning: in relation to a fraction; in relation to the specifics of fractions; as a nominator and denominator, instead of the word 'altogether', and for referring to a specific number.

Ernst-Slavit & Mason conclude by suggesting that 'the lack of awareness of the language demands of the content areas is a problem that deserves particular attention, especially when it comes to mainstream and content area teachers' and that 'teachers of ELLs will need to monitor their own language use and that of their students to provide the necessary verbal and non-verbal support structure for class participation and learning' (p. 438). ▨

Supporting or Hindering Language Learning

Clearly, as teachers, we need to be conscious of the needs of our students, particularly language learners and provide support, especially in ways to enable them to both develop understanding and demonstrate their ability, sometimes by means other than linguistic. In primary schools this may include engaging students in hands-on and practical activities such as art, cooking, science, and outdoor education, which has the added bonus for those in the stage of early childhood of supporting their cognitive development. We also need to incorporate pedagogical approaches that support language learners' development—helping meaning to be clearer, and using appropriate teaching strategies so that learners can make meaning themselves and, in doing so, move along their own interlanguage continuum.

According to Tabors & Snow (1994) this continuum of second language acquisition for children who commence learning the language after age three consists of a four-stage developmental sequence:

1   Home Language Use—despite their recognition that some people around them are using a different language, learners continue to use their home language to speak

2   Non-verbal Period—learners use gestures, facial expressions, and other non-verbal means in order to interact. This enables them to be part of the learning environment, and receive valuable input about the target language

3   Telegraphic and Formulaic Speech—this parallels a similar stage in first language acquisition where learners express themselves using just one or two words and by formulaic speech, such as 'You wannaplay'

4   Productive Language Use—children can produce language without relying on formulaic speech and although errors are still apparent, they are usually quite comprehensible

Teachers need to be conscious of where leaners are developmentally and provide conditions that optimize their acquisition. For example, they can provide a secure and welcoming environment when learners are at stage one; give students the opportunity to participate non-verbally when they are at stage two; and for students at stage three, they can recast in response to telegraphic speech (for example, when the student points to a snowman while doing a phonic matching activity and says, 'a man and snow,' and the teacher responds, 'Yes, it's a snowman.' (Oliver, unpublished data). At stage four, teachers can provide situations for their students that enable the production of comprehensible output, with opportunities for feedback. However, teachers need more than just an awareness of where learners are developmentally. Spotlight Study 3.3 illustrates how teachers can support and sometimes hinder language learning through classroom practices.

Spotlight Study 3.3

In a four-year study of two cohorts of ESL learners (six children in one and five in the other) from kindergarten to Grade 2 classes in Canada, Toohey & Day (1999) found many classroom practices that supported language learning for children at different stages of language development. For example, choral speech, songs, and rhymes used by teachers enabled L2 learners to appropriate new language over time, and to join in with other children.

In the following excerpts from one kindergarten lesson, we see that the teacher provides opportunities for recycling of language in this way. After reading the children a story of a dinosaur and a boy, the teacher prepares them to draw their own story book, repeatedly using the comparative 'bigger than'. Different children volunteer the completion of her sentence. When the children are later busy drawing, some are singing to themselves, rehearsing the same language again. Even those with minimal English, like Hari, are able to join in and be part of the classroom community in this way.

Whole class interaction

1 **Teacher:**   =than something. Paula, what else is the dinosaur bigger than?
2 **Paula:**   Urn squirrel.
3 **Teacher:**   Are bigger than a squirrel.
4 **Some children:** =Squirrel!=
5 **Teacher:**   =Sally, a dinosaur is bigger than.
6 **Sally:**   Urn a person.
7 **Teacher:**   A person oh let's see what mine. Some dinosaurs are bigger than?

Seat work [drawing]

1 **Joanna:**   Bigger than a house [then starts singing softly] bigger than a a tree? Bigger than a mama like a teddy bear bigger than a horse.
2 **Paula:**   What is that?
3 **Joanna:**   [singing] Bigger than a house bigger than a elephant.
4 **Paula:**   Bigger than the grass.
5 **Joanna:**   [singing] Bigger than a pencil crayon and bigger than a Joanna. [humming]

(Toohey & Day, 1999, pp. 45–46)

Conversely, other classroom interaction patterns seemed to interfere with children's opportunities to learn the language. For example, during whole class interaction, the teacher often required one child to speak at a time, and this could be difficult for the L2 learners, forcing them to display their flawed and minimal English. Further, they could not benefit from the assistance of peers, as seen in this excerpt, in which the teacher asks Surjeet to display knowledge of the food groups.

1 **Teacher:**   No Surjeet. It's not on the ceiling dear. It's right up here in front of you. Tell me the name of one food group, one of the four food groups …
2 **Surjeet:**   [quietly] Apple?
3 **Teacher:**   Surjeet I need the name of the entire food group. Apple is part of a particular food group. The names are written right there dear. They're printed right there. All you need to do is read it dear … What's the name of that food group that apple belongs to?
4 **Surjeet:**   [answers very quietly]
5 **Teacher:**   I can't hear you honey a little louder.
6 **Surjeet:**   Veg-e-tables veg-e-tables.
7 **Teacher:**   Pardon me? [leans forward] … What is an apple dear?
8 **Surjeet:**   Fruit.
9 **Teacher:**   An apple is a fruit so it belongs to the fruit and?
10 **Surjeet:**   Vegetables.
11 **Teacher:**   Thank you dear. The fruit and vegetable group.

(Toohey & Day, 1999, p. 47) ■

Supporting Language Learners: Language Understanding and Use

Developing understanding and language use are key roles for all teachers, and particularly so for those helping second language learners. When the language used at home is the same as the one used at school and parents have also received education in a school environment, students are often supported linguistically, cognitively, and academically. When it is not the same, and particularly when there is some 'distance' linguistically, that is, when students need to learn new linguistic cues and patterns of interaction used by different language and ethic groups (Au, 1980, 1985; Heath, 1983; Wong Fillmore, 1985), then the learning at school may be more difficult. Take, for example, the situation related to 'number'. This is a concept that has particular currency in Western cultures and it is reflected in the words we use (numbers, 'more', 'less', 'fewer', 'greater', etc.) and what we do, especially in school (for example, counting, comparing, measuring). However, in many indigenous cultures the concept of number is quite foreign, having little relevance to their traditional values and lifestyle. Thus, language features that refer to number will be more difficult to acquire than they would be for a child whose linguistic and cultural background is European. Therefore, the response that a young Australian Aboriginal student gives her teacher in Classroom Snapshot 3.8 is not surprising.

Classroom Snapshot 3.8

1 **Teacher:**   How many buckets of seeds will it take to fill up the seed bin for the chickens?

2 **Student:**   Big mob Miss.

(Oliver, Grote, Rochecouste & Exell, unpublished data)

Note that 'mob' in Aboriginal English is a word used to describe more than just a handful, so the expression 'Big mob' used by the student in this example was indication of a considerable number—but not an estimated number as the teacher was seeking.

Clearly there is a need for support to develop the learners' understanding and use of classroom-related language and the concepts underpinning this. However, as teachers we do need to exercise some caution with the language support we provide to language learners. For example, sometimes in an effort to help understanding, teachers provide reduced or restricted input to learners and because of this learners have limited opportunities to hear the specialized language of the content areas (Ernst-Slavit & Mason, 2011).

To counter this Gibbons (2006) suggests providing scaffolding for learners' language (see Chapter 2) so that they are introduced to and supported in their understanding and use of more complex and academic language.

As we described in Chapter 2, scaffolding from a learning perspective is simply a means of getting the support needed to complete a task that would be too complex to attempt independently (Pea, 2004; Wood, Bruner, & Ross, 1976). It is particularly important for young second language learners because of their stage of cognitive development—they may need scaffolding not just in terms of language, but also for conceptual understanding. It may also work to help maintain their concentration, and to enable them not to give up when the task seems too hard.

Classroom Snapshot 3.9 shows an example of scaffolding in a primary school context involving a six-year-old child, Yessara, who as yet speaks little English, working with an adult parent helper. The helper assists Yessara to carry out the class task, writing about pets, by first engaging her orally through a series of questions. The questions provide her with the majority of the language she needs for her writing, including how she can structure it.

Classroom Snapshot 3.9

1	**Helper:**	Lovely what have you written about your cat Kate? [reading the child's story] 'This is a cat and I love my cat.' Have you got a cat Y?
2	**Yessara:**	No.
3	**Helper:**	No your XX=
4	**Yessara:**	=dog
5	**Helper:**	You got a dog! What's its name?
6	**Yessara:**	Spot.
7	**Helper:**	Spot the dog! [laughs] What color's your dog?
8	**Yessara:**	Black.
9	**Helper:**	Is it a black dog! And do you play with it?
10	**Yessara:**	Yeah.
11	**Helper:**	What do you play with your dog?
12	**Yessara:**	A do= do= a ball.
13	**Helper:**	You play with a ball I bet your dog likes that.

(Philp, unpublished data) ▧

In this way, by scaffolding production, the helper was able to help the learner to say what she could not say unassisted, which in turn has supported her language use and potentially her development.

Language Learners and Socialization

As well as supporting the language required for academic success, teachers of younger children also need to help them develop the language for social success at school. In fact, Wong Fillmore & Snow (2000) describe one of the key roles of teachers as being an 'Agent of Socialization' (p. 11). This includes learning such things as taking turns, using greetings, and generally being polite. Further, this socialization includes learning how to participate in the conversations required for formal learning, 'not only what to say, but also how to say it' (Cekaite, 2007, p. 54).

Of course, such socialization is not restricted to second language learners, it is a need for most young children. However, it is a task that may be even more challenging when language is a barrier or when cultural practices at home or in previous classroom experience are 'distant' from what is expected.

Clearly one role for us as teachers is to help language learners acquire what is needed for classroom learning, and in many ways this language reflects the culture embedded within the curriculum. It is, therefore, incumbent upon us as teachers, particularly primary school teachers, to help develop our students' ability to navigate this part of the classroom. This includes helping them not only to develop the type of conceptual language required for the academic content of school—such as understanding and using number (as shown in Classroom Snapshot 3.8)—but also coming to understand and use the language that reflects the beliefs, values, and behavior of the education system in which they are operating. Classroom Snapshots 3.10 and 3.11 show the risks of assuming that students know and embrace those beliefs, values, and behavior.

Classroom Snapshot 3.10

1 **Teacher:**   You mustn't look at your partner's answer!
2 **Student:**   But she do good answer Miss.

(Oliver, Grote, Rochecouste, & Exell, unpublished data)

Classroom Snapshot 3.11

Amy (L1 Chinese) is drawing a picture on a piece of paper on Adam's (L1 Polish) desk.

1 **Ms Jones:**   Oh no Amy you're supposed to do that on your own. Everybody needs to do this sheet on their own. I need to know what everybody can do on their own.

2 **Luke:**   Ms Jones can I help Rita?
3 **Ms Jones:** No.
  [Luke then goes to Rita's desk]
4 **John:**   [classmate sitting next to Rita] [to Luke] Ms Jones said no.

[Luke sits on a bench near Rita]

5 **John:**   I'm keeping my eye on you.

[Linda comes up to teacher who is talking to an aide]

6 **Linda:**   Ms Jones Surjeet was helping Tiffany.
7 **Ms Jones:** Thank you Linda. Surjeet do your own work.
8 **Natalie:** Ms Jones Terry and Amy are looking at our work.
9 **Ms Jones:** Maybe you could move.

(Toohey, 1998, p. 75) ▨

By engaging in interaction, learners have the opportunity to benefit linguistically and socially from what others do with language. Further, through their participation they can imitate and build upon the language they hear and within the context of the exchange learn to use language appropriately.

Oral Interaction and Print Literacy

Clearly, developing oral language proficiency is important for a number of reasons, including for academic success, socialization, and for future success more generally. Developing print literacy—learning to read and write—is often considered even more important and is a key focus for most school systems and for many teachers of younger learners. However, what is sometimes overlooked is the enormous contribution of oral interaction to the success of developing print literacy (August & Shanahan, 2006). Thus, alongside literacy instruction, there is need for extensive oral English development in our classrooms.

As we saw in Classroom Snapshot 2.1, when the teacher discussed the word 'bony' taken from the class reading book, oral interaction enabled the students to develop better understanding of the vocabulary of the text they were reading. It is not vastly different from the approach that many teachers of young learners use for developing literacy in a child's first language. In fact, Hudelson (1994) suggests that, particularly for children, there are many similarities in the process of becoming literate in first and second languages because, regardless of language, they need to learn how the set of symbols on the page represents meaning and how they can decode this to understand what is written. Like many others, Hudelson recommends a classroom environment that promotes the use of collaborative learning, and the use of oral (and written) personal narratives. Making the link between literacy activities and content learning explicit through understandable classroom talk is also important. Not only do these activities support literacy in a general way, but they also provide access to the type of interaction that supports second language learning (as discussed in Chapter 2).

Interaction between Peers in the Primary School Classroom

From what we have described so far, it is clear that teachers have a vital role to play in assisting language learners. Even so, as we have also outlined, the one-to-many situation of a teacher and class can be restrictive and therefore using the interaction between peers is another way to facilitate learning, especially second language learning (for example, Dörnyei & Murphy, 2003). When engaging in peer interaction there is a real need to communicate and, unlike the situation in classroom discussions, there is less opportunity for the individual to 'opt out' of the discussion. Peers working together create a situation where they must 'grapple with the target language at a more challenging level' (Philp, Oliver, & Mackey, 2008, p. 12).

Benefits

One of the advantages of peer interaction, especially in primary school classes, is that the learners are at a similar stage of cognitive and social development (Damon & Phelps, 1989; Hartup, 1989). As teachers we may have encountered the situation where we have tied ourselves in knots trying unsuccessfully to explain something to a student in a class. Despite reformulating and illustrating in the most concrete of ways, the child simply does not understand what we are saying. Minutes of valuable class time seem to be wasted as we dig ourselves into a verbal 'black hole'. Then as frustration levels rise, another student provides the simplest of explanations and suddenly understanding is achieved. Peers are a valuable resource because they are at a similar stage of development and often have a better understanding of why a classmate might not 'get it'. In addition, the explainer also benefits—having to teach someone else often clarifies things for the child as tutor. Thus, as with first language learning, peer interaction in the second language classroom includes social, cultural, academic, and affective benefits (Philp, Adams, & Iwashita, 2013). For instance, one of the key benefits peers provide is motivation: peers help to make learning fun. Of particular importance to this book are the beneficial opportunities peers provide in terms of second language acquisition.

Peer Contributions to Social and Academic Success

Like teachers, peers have an important role to play in the socialization process of language learners. Hartup (1989, p. 112) describes how peers can help 'elaborate these skills (social skills) with individuals who are more or less similar to themselves'. This affiliation that is developed through peer interaction is a key part of children's social development. Further, as children progress from early to late childhood (corresponding to the upper primary years), because of their own desire and development they spend increasingly more time with their peers, and less with adults, and this continues to increase in teenage years, as we will see in Chapter 4.

When young children begin school they need to learn to collaborate with others in formal and informal ways. Providing opportunities for peer interaction, such as pair-work and group-work, certainly encourages such development. Therefore peer interaction can complement the interactional benefits of teacher–student interaction (Philp, Adams, & Iwashita, 2013) and in turn this supports language learning and contributes to academic success. Therefore, as teachers we need to create opportunities for our students to work in groups or pairs in both formal and informal ways. This may include having students complete hands-on activities, for instance, in math, doing graphing activities together, or in science, working in teams planting seeds and measuring and recording the growth of plants in different conditions. For younger children, as we have seen in our snapshots, it might be as simple as having the children play together with building blocks. It might also involve informal role-play in the dress-up corner. Taking such an approach enhances opportunities for oral interaction, whilst still enabling content to be covered (Corson, 2001).

However, interactional opportunities among peers can be both positive and negative. For example, after a year-long study of four children in a first grade class, Willett (1995) found that they often tried to appear competent and like the other children in the class, through use of formulaic utterances. Three girls, working together, managed this with much greater success than the single boy who was isolated from his peers. Similarly, Toohey (2000), describing elementary (K-3) classrooms, and Barnard (2009), in a study of an upper primary (year 5) classroom, both remark on the differential success of the second language learners in classrooms—some of whom were helped and others hindered by classroom practices that allowed them to make use of the resources of more capable peers, or prevented from doing so through such factors as seating arrangements. These studies also suggest that some children are unable to participate as members of the classroom community when they are not given the social support of their peers. In these studies, we see that peer talk is crucial, not only as a source of target language input, but also because it provides the context in which children can form friendships, align themselves with others, and gain the motivation and context for L2 use (Philp & Duchesne, 2008). Therefore, teachers need to consider carefully how they construct settings and task conditions in order to foster those interactions that enable supportive peer interaction.

In addition, and although the importance of peer interaction is generally well recognized, some teachers may feel that in the beginning years of primary school, second language learners are too young to work effectively with their peers. Certainly they need to be introduced to doing so in carefully staged ways. Like all classroom events, tasks involving peer interaction may not run smoothly; however, it is possible. Oliver's 2009 study, conducted with quite newly arrived second language learning children aged 5–7 years, demonstrates that, when interacting with their peers, this age group was able to negotiate for meaning, and to provide and use corrective feedback in a way that adult language learners do. However, there were some qualitative differences in their interaction, reflecting their stage of development. For instance, they could be liberal with the truth and they were, at times, quite egocentric; they also seemed 'less bound by the content and strictures of the task' (p. 148). See, for example, Classroom Snapshot 3.12 where, after a protracted exchange to determine the correct location to place a picture of a loaf of bread, Marion simply decides to place it where she likes.

Classroom Snapshot 3.12

1	**Marion:**	Put in the= the=
2	**Sally:**	=Pick up what?
3		A bread?
4	**Marion:**	Huh?
5	**Sally:**	Pick up a bread?
6	**Marion:**	Um bread?
7		No I don't have a bread.
8		Have you a= oh sorry [locates picture of bread]
9		Um put it where?
10	**Sally:**	In the bread.
11	**Marion:**	Huh?

12 **Sally:**   In the table.
13   Table.
14 **Marion:**   No I want to put in the= in the bread I like here. [points to a
                different position for the bread]

(Oliver, 2009a, p. 148) ▨

Although the younger children in Classroom Snapshot 3.12 were creative in the way they solved the set task, they still interacted in socially appropriate ways. They were also able to collaborate in a manner that facilitated their learning, so that they benefitted socially and academically from each other in the process.

Because of their essential equality, children provide a different sort of support than teachers do. They share common interests and fascinations, similar levels of physical and social ability (Duchesne et al., 2013), though they are not always equivalent in L2 proficiency. Because of this they can explore and experiment with language together. However, as we indicated with teacher interaction, the type of learning that occurs when peers interact is somewhat dictated by the nature of the task. Coughlan & Duff (1994), for instance, found that even how learners approach the task and whether they consider it an interactive task or not, affects how the interaction occurs and whether or not they use such communicative strategies such as negotiation. Despite what we do know about peer interaction and its potential to contribute to second language learning, with the limited amount of research undertaken with children thus far, there is much more yet to do.

Peers Supporting SLA through Interaction

Not only are peers an important resource for social and academic learning, but as we suggested in Chapter 2 they serve as an important resource for second language learning. This is as true for children as it is for those who are older. This is because in many ways they can potentially act as teachers of the same age (Mercer, 1995). For example, Oliver (2000) found that child ESL learners were just as likely as their adult counterparts to use feedback provided by their partners. In a similar way, Mackey, Oliver, & Leeman (2003) found that there were more opportunities for partners in peer interaction to provide each other with useful interactional feedback (of the type described in Chapter 2) than occurred in whole class interactions, and in fact, children were more likely to make use of this feedback than were adult learners.

Peer interaction in primary school classrooms is a valuable context for language practice (Corson, 2001; Tognini, Philp, & Oliver, 2010). We see this in Classroom Snapshot 3.13, where a pair of primary school-aged children are practicing naming colors whilst describing furniture pieces in French. Their conversation is stilted and not always target like, but their practice may contribute to fluency development and recall of key vocabulary. Most importantly they appear to be having fun.

Classroom Snapshot 3.13

1 **A:** *La Frigidaire ... est ... jaune?* [laughter] [The fridge ... is ... yellow?]
2 **M:** *Non. La commode ... est ... mauve?* [No. The chest ... is ... purple?]
3 **A:** *Errm ... la commode ... jaune?* [Errm ... the chest ... yellow?]
4 **M:** *No. Le divan ...* [mispronounced 'divin'] [No. The couch ...]

(Tognini, Philp, & Oliver, 2010, p. 28.12) ▦

Peers for Fun and Play

Whether in foreign language or second language settings, what is particularly important for children is that peer interaction is a context in which they get to take risks, be silly, and have fun with language. Further, they can use language in ways that would seem quite inappropriate for adults. This may include using language play—having fun with language, its sound and form, and doing so in ways that adults are unlikely to do. For example, in our data collection for a study about peer interaction, we found the word 'octagon' was repeated endlessly and with great gusto, eventually almost by the whole ESL class of 6- and 7-year-olds. One child started it simply through the request to a partner ('How many octagons can you see?') on a pair-work task. The partner repeated the word, the original child repeated the word again, they repeated it together, pairs nearby started to repeat it—they simply had fun—enjoying the sense and feel of the new word as it tripped off their tongues. These children were at a similar stage of development— the fun they had with a word that appealed to them would have been unlikely with older learners.

Fun, especially with words, is often in the ear of the beholder—as seen in Classroom Snapshot 3.14.

Classroom Snapshot 3.14

1 **R:** I've got a sticker.
2 **S:** I've got a sticker.

3 **Y:** Hey Roberta.
4 **S:** Hey Roberta I'll tell you something.
5 **Y:** Rubber rubber.
6 **S:** Rubber rubber rubber. [imitating rolled /r/ of Y]
7 **R:** Rub rub rubber.
8 **S:** Rubber rubber rubber. [attempting rolled /r/ without success]

(Philp & Duchesne, 2008, p. 95) ■

In addition to language play, play involving language, such as pretend play in early primary years, offers unique opportunities for language use, practice, and development. Ervin-Tripp (1991) describes pretend play as a context for language learning as 'a rich source of important language practice in different styles and vocabulary … it provides a chance to practice a range of speech acts, styles and registers' (p. 88). In this context, children can practice using language outside their normal experience for use. For example, when they imagine themselves as a teacher, a father, or an ambulance driver, they get to adopt a unique tone, specialized vocabulary, and a social register they do not get to use as a child. Language in this play-acting is often supported by the structure of a familiar scenario (for example, the teacher in the classroom, the doctor and her patient, the shopkeeper and his customer) and often, by real or pretend props (Fassler 1998; Philp, Adams, & Iwashita, 2013). In classroom settings, these scenarios might involve real-world or fictional characters. Among older children, such play-acting can become more formalized (such as a school performance, or dramatic enactments associated with a curriculum theme). Together, such imaginative play provides a rich resource for second language learning. It is certainly something teachers of primary school learners can incorporate as part of the second language learning experience. For example, setting up a shop in the classroom allows learners to have fun playing 'shopping', whilst at the same time allowing opportunities for practice (for example, names of different food, numbers and money), thus contributing to second language development.

Role of First Language

All educators need to support second language learners as they enter school, and recognize that they need to help their students develop the social, cultural, and academic language that is appropriate for the classroom. Of key importance is an understanding that such endeavors take time to achieve. Of equal importance is an understanding that such development should not be at the expense of the home language—what is described in the literature as **subtractive bilingualism** (Lambert, 1975). That is, the language of school should not replace the home language. Instead we need to promote the maintenance of the home language alongside the learning of the additional 'school' language. In fact, we need to promote strong and healthy communication in the home language because, as Cummins (2000) has outlined, our second language proficiency is strongly aligned to our proficiency in our first. Within our classrooms we need to demonstrate an appreciation of home language, and ask genuine questions about students' language and culture such as: 'How would you say this?', 'Do you do have something similar in your family?', 'Do you have a similar custom/tradition/ activity in your culture … tell us about it'. Such inclusive practices are not only helpful for the learners, but also contribute to the education of all students—and their teachers!

Children's use of their first language is not only important for communication within the family. As Cummins (2000) and others suggest, it also a natural and beneficial part of second language learning. For example, in their study of immersion classrooms, Swain & Lapkin (2000) outline three reasons for first language use:

1   Most commonly, students may use their first language to move the task along, such as getting started and managing the language and organizational aspects of the task
2   It can help to focus attention, especially on aspects of vocabulary and grammar
3   Students may use it for interpersonal interaction, such as during disagreements or when engaging in off-task discussion and social chit-chat

As children get older, another important function of first language use emerges, namely as a way to signal group identity (Blanco-Iglesias, Broner, & Tarone, 1995; Tarone & Swain, 1995). Whilst normally associated with teenage behavior, Blanco-Iglesias et al. found that, for reasons related to group identity, students' use of their first language began to emerge at around nine and ten years. Similar findings for the positive benefits of the first language have been reported in other second language learning contexts (Platt & Brooks, 1994; Brooks, Donato, & McGone, 1997; Antón & DiCamilla, 1998).

Some years ago, when we began language teaching, the use of first language in second- or foreign-language classrooms was frowned upon. It was thought that using the learners' L1 would reduce the amount of

L2 input to learners and decrease their chances of acquiring the target language. Nowadays, however, we understand that first language can and does have a positive role to play in second language classrooms and this is as true for primary school learners as it is for those who are older.

Summary

In this chapter we have seen that primary school-aged children have different needs and abilities from their older counterparts—although they are ultimately likely to reach higher levels of second language skill than those who start their language-learning journey later in life. However, at least in terms of interaction, there are also some similarities: for example, as with older school students, the context of younger students' language learning will influence the type of interaction that occurs, including the type of feedback that is provided and then used.

As teachers planning for second language learning in the primary school classroom, we need to take into account the needs of younger learners, including their stage of cognitive and social development. Within school, the formality and complexity of classroom interaction may present particular challenges for primary school-aged learners and, depending on their cultural background and experiences, this may be a greater challenge for some than for others. However, there are things we can do as teachers to help. For example, scaffolding will assist not only with language learning, but also with understanding the content of different subjects and the social practices used in classrooms. Similarly, peer interaction that is motivating and fun can be used effectively to support second language learning. Finally, the use of a learner's first language can make a positive contribution to learning in general and to second language learning in particular.

4

Oral Interaction in the High School Classroom Context: Research and Implications for Pedagogy

Preview

In this chapter, we explore oral interaction in the high school classroom context. We will begin by briefly considering some of the particular strengths of adolescents as language learners, and some of the challenges they may face. We are especially interested in answering the following questions:

- What are the characteristics of high school learners?
- What types of oral interactions are high school learners engaged in?
- How does interaction contribute to learning language in the high school context?
- Do individual learner characteristics make a difference to language learning success?

As we explore these questions we will be considering the implications of our answers for teaching practice.

Adolescents as Language Learners

High school-aged learners are adolescents in the period of development between childhood and adulthood (Duchesne et al., 2013), at a time where there is quite a distinct social context. With increased self-sufficiency and independence, students at this age may spend greater amounts of time among their peers than with family members and other adults, and in a wider range of social settings than home and school. This greater reliance on peers is often reflected in behavioral and language choices (Philp, Adams, & Iwashita, 2013; Berk, 2013). Adolescence is also a time of unique cognitive, social, and emotional development associated with the biological changes of puberty. This typically begins in the early high school years, but can occur in the late primary school years—and for this reason, some of our discussion is also relevant to children of this age.

In many ways, adolescents could be considered to be at the height of their ability to learn languages, particularly in instructional settings, whereas younger learners may have the edge in informal contexts, as we noted in Chapter 3. High school students' advanced cognitive, social, and linguistic abilities foster new learning opportunities (Berk, 2013; Muñoz 2003, 2007). For example, these older learners have the capacity to think abstractly and make logical inferences; they also have the ability to deal with more complex content, and to use the appropriate language for talking about it.

Metalinguistic Ability

By high school, students have also developed the metalinguistic ability to think about language form and how it works (Berman, 2007) and are able to articulate this (Oliver, Haig, & Rochecouste, 2004, 2005). This can be seen in Classroom Snapshot 4.1, where two high school students are working out instructions for a recipe in Italian. Student I notices two different ways of saying 'the' (*il* or *la*); student K provides an explanation and although she doesn't use grammatical terms (such as 'masculine' or 'feminine ending' on the noun), what she says does reflect an awareness of patterns in the language.

Classroom Snapshot 4.1

1 **Student I:** Why is it why is it *il* or *la*? I don't understand it.
2 **Student K:** Because it ends in 'a' it's *la* and 'o' it's *il*.
3 **Student I:** Oh I get it. *Grattugiano … grattugiano il cioccolato.*
   [struggles with where to put the stress on the word 'grattugiano'] [Grate the chocolate.]

(Tognini, Philp, & Oliver, 2010, p. 28.16, annotation added) ▦

Philp, Adams, & Iwashita (2013) argue that, because of this 'greater metalinguistic awareness, there is greater potential to focus on form-related difficulties, to articulate them and reflect upon them' (p. 114). However, as seen above, this does not mean they necessarily use linguistic terms to describe it. As we will see later in this chapter, this ability suggests that it is worthwhile for teachers to draw learners' attention to particular patterns in language. Adolescents' ability to talk about language in a decontextualized way can actually help them recognize these patterns and apply this knowledge to generate new sentences of their own.

In a series of studies of students learning English as a foreign language in Canada (Quebec) and in Spain, White (2008) and her colleagues explored the difficulty many learners have in working out whether to say 'his' or 'her' in English (White & Ranta, 2002; White, Muñoz, & Collins, 2007). These researchers compared different ways of helping French-speaking learners aged 11–14 years. They found that teaching the learners 'a rule of thumb' for possessives helped them the most (for example, 'Ask yourself whose ____ is it?'). For example, one student wrote 'her' in a cloze sentence: 'David's mother prepared the cake for ____ son's party'. When he explained why he'd chosen to say 'her' (not 'his'), he used the rule of thumb exemplified previously: 'Because whose son is it? Is the mother, at the mother's' (White, 2008, p. 214).

Social Development

In addition to greater metalinguistic awareness, adolescents also have superior social skills. This means that group-work at this age can provide a highly productive context for exploring and using language. They can cooperate with one another, negotiate disagreements themselves, and efficiently organize to work collaboratively. On the other hand, it is also important to recognize the difficulties that can arise in group-work—at this age, social, psychological, and emotional factors can hinder the potential for learning. Because of peer pressure or low self-esteem, learners may feel inhibited to talk for fear of embarrassment or ridicule, or be unwilling to take risks in language learning. It is also a time when individuals are exploring issues related to their self-identity and this, too, can impact on their willingness to interact in social and more formal contexts.

Interaction in the High School Mainstream Classroom: L2 settings

Clearly, there is uniqueness about adolescent learners. Characteristics particular to this age group can impact on the way they engage orally with their teacher and their peers in classrooms where they are learning a second language while also learning the content of their academic subjects, either in mainstream classrooms or in special programs designed to prepare them for the mainstream.

Activity 4.1

Think of a classroom where adolescents are learning both a new language and new academic content. In the table below, take a moment to note down your own thoughts in response to following two questions:

- What types of interaction do we see in secondary school classrooms?
- How can these interactions assist language learning?

Some ideas are included as examples.

Examples of interaction	How this assists learning
Peer interaction	
Students work out an oral text together for example, making up a story, poem, or description	1 Opportunity to experiment with how to express things in the L2 2
	1 Fun and motivating L2 use 2
Semi-scripted role play in pairs	1 Opportunity to practice new language, and develop use of formulaic language 2 Helps learners' fluency and accuracy in use of specific grammatical forms
Teacher-student interaction	
Teacher leads class to explain the results of a science experiment	1 Scaffolds language production by providing structure, models and new vocabulary 2 Enables learners to articulate results before writing a report themselves
Teacher discusses a reading text with the class and highlights key vocabulary	1 Helps guide reading and comprehension through discussion of key ideas 2
	1 Provides feedback on students' production 2

Photocopiable © Oxford University Press

Table 4.1 Types and benefits of interaction in a classroom

Challenges of Mastering CALP and BICS

As we noted in Chapter 1, second language learners need to gain mastery over both academic language (CALP) and general oral proficiency (BICS) to succeed in schools, and this can take years to develop (two to five years for BICS and four to seven years for CALP) in second language settings (Cummins, 2000; Hakuta, Butler, & Witt, 2000). This is at the heart of many of the challenges for immigrant learners in an L2 mainstream context and can also be true for learners in a Content-Based Language Teaching class. They need to master both academic content and the language that goes with it, and are likely to lag behind native speaker peers in this mastery. They also need to acculturate to a new community, especially to their age peers both inside and outside of the classroom. Oral proficiency is key to achieving this. In this section we will consider the challenges of both CALP and BICS, of both mastering academic content and becoming part of a new language community, and how classroom interaction may help in the context of high school.

In formal high school classrooms, across all subjects, adolescents are expected to develop greater linguistic proficiency, expanding on their productive and receptive language use (Berman, 2007). This will occur with their increasing awareness of linguistic registers, both oral and written, and as they gain greater control over their linguistic repertoire and their ability to understand and reproduce different discourse styles. For second language learners, this challenge is particularly acute because their control of the target language and their general linguistic repertoire (for example, receptive and productive vocabulary knowledge) is often very limited. One way in which learners can negotiate these difficulties is through careful scaffolding by the teacher. Another is through practicing in oral interaction with peers. We will look at each in turn.

Contribution of Teacher–Student Interaction in Classrooms

For adolescent learners to develop their oral interaction abilities in high school classrooms, it is helpful for there to be an explicit focus on technical and low frequency words in subject areas, coupled with opportunities to then use those terms productively. This is exemplified in Classroom Snapshot 4.2 below. In this high school economics class in New Zealand, the teacher explains the concepts of appreciation and depreciation to describe changes in value. He draws the students' attention to how to express this in a number of ways: he writes the key vocabulary items on the board, and also gives visual symbols of the core meaning; he stresses the words and says them slowly to the class; he repeats the words a number of times, and rephrases them ('It's gone up'); and he illustrates the use of the words in sentences that relate to knowledge the students were already familiar with (the state of the New Zealand dollar).

Classroom Snapshot 4.2

Teacher says:	Teacher writes on board:
So there might be the word like … 'appreciation'	Appreciation
You can have it like 'appreciating' as well>	Appreciating
So you can actually say it in a sentence. We can use it in here [teacher points to an answer on the board that he had elicited earlier]	NZ $ 1 = US $ 0.80
and say 'The New Zealand dollar is appreciating' or you can say it in a sentence 'The New Zealand dollar has appreciated.' OK? It's gone up over the last week	value ↑
or 'There has been an appreciation of the New Zealand dollar.' What's the opposite to appreciation? … OK depreciation	depreciation ↓

(From DVD, Ministry of Education, New Zealand, 2008) ■

As Berman (2007) notes, it is in high school that learners start to become more familiar with adjectives like 'considerable' and 'industrial' that are more scholarly terms rather than everyday terms such as 'dirty' and 'sunny' (p. 350), and oral interaction can give students practice at using these in context. In this lesson, students were exposed to the key technical terms of their subject area through the input of the teacher, and then were given the opportunity to use the terms themselves in a subsequent pair-work task (shown in Classroom Snapshot 4.3). They later moved from talking about exchange rates to writing about them. Talking it through first helped them understand the key concepts and to apply their understanding by solving problems with a partner. It also helped them articulate these ideas more clearly, using appropriate terms, before having to write a report individually.

Peer Interaction in L2 Settings

It is important to recognize peer interaction as a context for learning in the classroom. Philp, Adams, & Iwashita (2013) describe peer interaction as 'any communicative activity carried out between learners, where there is minimal or no participation from the teacher. This can include cooperative and collaborative learning, peer tutoring and other forms of help from peers' (p. 3). Peer interaction often complements the work of the teacher with the whole class. Researchers in educational psychology (for example, Damon & Phelps, 1989; Hartup, 1992; O'Donnell, 2006; Topping & Ehly, 1998) believe that the benefits of learning through working with peers stem partly from their essential equality. In contrast to the teacher who has specialist knowledge, superior proficiency, higher status, and different viewpoints as an adult, peers typically share a relatively similar status—what they think or say is open for negotiation, their knowledge, language, and viewpoint are often congruent—and a peer might be able to explain something in a way that makes more sense. Hence, pair- and group-work can provide a context in which to practice language they are uncertain of and try out options in a less public arena, and without the teacher's correction. Similarly, students may seek the help of a friend, in whispers on the side, rather than ask the teacher—not wishing their ignorance to be exposed.

Classroom Snapshot 4.3 provides an example of this practice aspect of peer interaction. As we saw in Classroom Snapshot 4.2, the economics teacher had prepared learners for oral interaction in pairs by explaining the task and highlighting key language and concepts. This snapshot shows a later conversation between two students in the same economics class as they work on a barrier task. They each hold a picture of six graphs showing supply and demand rates. Amy, a Korean student, has been in the school for three years. Her partner, Lucy, is a New Zealander. They take turns to describe a graph that matches a particular situation. In this case, Amy provides the description while her partner identifies which of the six graphs she is describing. Their interaction reflects the difficulties—both of content and language—that need to be negotiated. Having to describe and interpret the graph for a partner pushes Amy to try to understand the graph, and to articulate her thoughts more clearly. When her partner questions her interpretation, Amy has to re-think her description and realizes she is mistaken in her understanding. Although she makes many grammatical errors, what she says is clear to her partner. In this context, the learner receives feedback on content rather than on language.

Classroom Snapshot 4.3

1 **Amy:**   But if demand curve um increase then um exchange rate is increase as well? … So the export will be decrease isn't it?

2 **Lucy:**   I don't see how the exports could decrease.
3 **Amy:**   Mm so it's D I think.

(From DVD, Ministry of Education, New Zealand, 2008) ▨

After this class, Amy commented that having to describe the graph with her partner helped her to understand it better: 'Usually lecture-style lesson makes me lost my concentration on the lesson, but barrier exercise make me more concentrate on the exercise because it's not for myself it's it's also for my partner' (from DVD, Ministry of Education, New Zealand, 2008).

Oral Interaction and L2 Writing

In Chapter 3, we saw that for primary school learners, oral and written literacy often go hand in hand. The same is true for high school students. Oral interaction can facilitate L2 writing by enabling learners to first develop their ideas, work out the language they need to express those ideas, and then organize them into a coherent argument through oral language. This is illustrated in Spotlight Study 4.1.

Spotlight Study 4.1

In a study of minority-language students in two Canadian high school 'transitional' English literature classes, Early & Marshall (2008) looked at how the teacher (Marshall) helped learners to read, understand, and write about short story texts through a multi-modal approach. Instead of just reading and writing, the students were first required to engage with these texts through oral interaction and visual work. The researchers found that this helped the students to recognize elements of the texts they had not understood before, and more importantly, to start to understand and actually become interested in the stories.

Their study followed the progress of two classes over a month as students began to develop the ability to analyze written texts. The classes had 13–15 students, from Grades 8–11, with most at Grade 10. They were predominantly L1 Mandarin and Cantonese speakers, other languages spoken were: Farsi, Korean, Japanese, Russian, and Romanian. These students had great difficulty engaging with short stories written in English. To help the students think more about the stories, the teacher asked them to create mandalas (a learning tool adapted from Indian and Tibetan Buddhism). The students worked collaboratively in small groups to visually represent features of the short stories.

The mandalas served to give students a basic framework for identifying the theme, style, and characterization of a short story using visual symbols and written quotations from the text. This involved them in extensive discussions with one another, going back and forth between discussing, re-reading the text, and interpreting it visually and linguistically. In an interview, the teacher notes the learners' engagement in oral participation:

> I think there were huge amounts of communication. Trying to wrap your mind around the symbols of the mandala and trying to explain it to other people … that whole thing of putting out ideas, well, what about if we did this? Negotiating your way around ideas … around your ideas versus someone else's … there was a lot of language expression.
>
> (Early & Marshall, 2008, p. 389)

The students themselves felt that their conversations in groups gave them greater insight and understanding of the texts:

> Three heads are better than one … talking and arguing the ideas was really helpful to think deep, gets lots of different things … it was interesting to hear and to think, 'How did they get that? … I don't think that's what it means' … and talk about that.
>
> (Early & Marshall, 2008, p. 388)

In addition, the affective pleasure of working with peers was in itself motivating:

> It was great to show up and know that I have conversations with friends. We talked about the project the whole time. Sometimes I would think of an answer of something I didn't know in class. I would ask them right away.
>
> (Early & Marshall, 2008, p. 388)

This study emphasizes the way oral interaction can contribute to learning of both content and language. Employing a visual framework and a strong component of oral work helped push the learners to think through the characteristics of the text in ways they had been unable to do individually. Early & Marshall also emphasize that it was not only CALP that the students were developing, but also 'the complex interpersonal communicative proficiency necessary for school, work, and social success' (p. 389).

This study also reflects some of the challenges facing high school learners because of the complexity of the texts and tasks they encounter—these can be difficult in terms of both language and content. It also illustrates how oral interaction between peers can support learning. Working together in discussion and using visual cues helped these second language learners to understand content better. It also supported their reading and writing development. Through collaboration with peers they were able to put their thoughts into words informally, before having to write it in a more formal context, such as an essay. Thus the structure of the task (in this case, a mandala requiring three visual images and three quotes, each with a particular focus) helped scaffold the learners' understanding and language use. ▨

Negotiating a Place amongst Peers

So far we have seen that second language learners in mainstream contexts are faced with linguistic and content difficulties associated with academic discourse. Oral interactions with the teacher and with peers are ways that students can be assisted to resolve these difficulties. However, students also face the cultural and social challenges of negotiating their place in a high school community in a new country. Both teacher–student and peer interaction can promote or hinder this process.

Spotlight Study 4.2

In a study of high school classes in Canada, with both Canadian-born and immigrant students, Duff (2003) found that references to popular culture could be both positive but could also have negative consequences if not used thoughtfully. On the one hand, the teachers' use of popular culture and reference to well-known television characters, such as Bart Simpson, helped to engage L1 English students and to make the formal language of school more accessible to them. This is seen here, as the teacher explains the word 'serendipitous'.

1 **Teacher:** If something is serendipitous or if you uh are benefited= blessed
     with serendipity you mess something up.
2 **Sue:**   =Coincidental=
3 **Teacher:** =But it turns out to be the great=
4 **Jim:**   =Pull a Homer?
5 **Teacher:** It's what= it turns out. Good. Yeah you pull a Homer Simpson?
     Yeah. Exactly. So serendipitous. This is a serendipitous …
     serendipitous discovery just because she [the cancer researcher]
     wasn't able to get the uh things that she wanted …

(Duff, 2003, p. 232)

As the teacher explains the word 'serendipitous', a student, Jim, provides the phrase 'Pull a Homer' (line 4). The teacher latches on to this popular idiom—a reference to the US television program, *The Simpsons*. However, for students whose first language was not English, and who had little familiarity with these iconic characters, oblique references to pop culture served to widen the gap, and further marginalize them. The speed of the dialogue and the overlapping of turns we see between the teacher and the students (lines 2–4) also made it particularly difficult for these second language speakers to be included in the conversation.

Duff interviewed students from the class, and found that generally the L2 learners were reticent to speak up in class: one student, Alex, said, 'Canadian boys laugh; if I speak, some 'white people' won't understand; it's uncomfortable' (p. 255). They also reported having difficulty being able to participate in multi-party interactions that were too fast for them to make a contribution, as TN notes:

… Kind of difficult because we can't really speak English all the time. So they may not understand what we are talking about. So we are difficult to communicate … we need to organize in our brain to speak out English … [Instead] we just listen.

(TN, Hong Kong, 1.5 years in Canada) (Duff, 2003, p. 258)

Canadian native English-speaking students also noted a divide between the 'ESL students' and themselves:

A lot of them are amazing people who I could be very good friends with but there are things like language barriers and just really separate lives. There's no motivation to blend the two at all … And I think that might be one of the spots where um the segregation starts between ESL students and us because they don't have the same radio stations and they don't have the same they don't watch the same movies and … they're not as absorbed by the same pop culture that we are. You know? They have their own.

(SK) (Duff, 2003, p. 258)

In a similar way as outlined in Spotlight Study 4.2, Miller (2003), in a study of ten high school learners, aged 13–16 years in their first year in Australian high schools, reports a lack of connection between local students and newly arrived students. She found L2 learners were unwilling to talk in class and often unable to find any way 'in' to be accepted by local students. This represents another challenge for second language learners in high schools. In spite of the obvious potential benefits that friendship with L2 peers may hold, at this age, peers may act as gatekeepers, hindering inclusion in vital social networks. Miller found that many of the newcomers spent their time with other students who spoke the same L1, looked the same, and with whom they had more in common. This may help them to survive school, but also reduces opportunities to use the L2 with their peers, and makes it more difficult for them to gain mastery in L2 oral proficiency. This highlights the importance of fostering relationships between peers. The teacher may scaffold learners' L2 learning, but interaction with peers is also essential for social inclusion in the class and school community. These aspects of interaction are particular to mainstream classroom settings. In the next section, we consider aspects of interaction specific to foreign language settings.

Interaction in Foreign Language Settings

In this section we focus on the nature of oral interaction in foreign language settings, in which learners have far less target input and limited class time. In these settings, typically, both the teacher and the learners share a common first language, and this can be used to support L2 use.

Activity 4.2

Look at these two different examples from high school foreign language classrooms. Class A are learning Spanish in a private boarding high school for girls in the USA. Class B is a German class in a British high school.

For each one, can you identify the purpose of using the target language in the interaction?

Class A Teacher with whole class, learning Spanish

Teacher: All right … *a:* [glances through the book] … *Para la tarea quiero que escriban una composición a: de quince oraciones sobre lo que … a: sobre lo que hizo la sema el fin de semana pasado. Entonces m:es a:* … [writes on the board] As homework I want you to write an essay of 15 sentences about what you did last weekend.

F: Ay, Mr. T! We just did that or something like that last week.

Teacher: Drew! [writes on the board] … *Hay que practicar si quieres aprender el español hay que practicar* [continues writing on the board] You've got to practise if you want to learn Spanish you've got to practise.

(Lacorte, 2005, p. 393)

Class B Teacher with whole class, learning German

Teacher: *Wohin ist Ann gefahren?* [points to table on screen] [Where has Anne gone?] Mandy.

Mandy: *Sie ist nach Spanien gefahren.* [She has gone to Spain.]

Teacher: *Sie ist nach Spanien gefahren. Gut. Wohin ist Sandra gefahren?* [She has gone to Spain. Good. Where has Sandra gone?] Lynne.

Lynne: *Sie ist nach Frankreich gefahren.* [She has gone to France.]

Teacher: *Gut. Sie ist nach Frankreich gefahren.* [Good. She has gone to France.]

(Westgate, Batey, Brownlee, & Butler, 1985, p. 278, translation added)

These transcripts reflect two quite different roles for interaction. In both classrooms, the teacher uses the target language for the majority of the time. In Class A, the teacher uses the target language for everyday classroom purposes—for talking about homework, for encouraging the students to work harder. However, in contrast the students tend to use English for such purposes rather than the target language. In Class B, although the whole interaction is conducted in German, the language is very predictable and there is restrictive use of turn-taking. Here, there is little exchange of information since the answers are known to everyone (from the screen). Instead, oral interaction appears to be used solely to practice key language terms.

Roles for Interaction

A variety of types of interaction and the role this plays in learning are found in a number of descriptive studies by researchers of high school foreign language classrooms. For example, Erlam & Sakui (2006) undertook case studies of three classes (French and Japanese) in New Zealand high schools. Tognini (2008) looked at six classes (French and Italian) in Australia. In the UK, Mitchell & Martin (1997) observed the classes of five teachers of year-7 students over two semesters. In each of these studies, there were a number of similarities. Firstly, in terms of method of data collection: each used teacher and student interviews, as well as classroom observation. Another similarity was that all found that the greater amount of time in the class was spent on oral activities. Further, there was a mixture of both communicative language use (as seen in Class A above) and practice-oriented language use (as seen in Class B), with quite a variation in the amount of each according to the teacher. Not surprisingly, it appeared that teachers' beliefs, as garnered from the interviews, had a lot to do with this. There was also variation between teachers according to how much group-work was used and the extent to which the target language was the main medium of instruction. For example, in the beginning level language classrooms observed by Mitchell & Martin (1997), much of the interaction was teacher-centered rather than group-work, in order to maintain control and to provide L2 input. In other foreign language contexts, however, teachers may not have the oral proficiency or the confidence to use the target language as the main medium of instruction.

Patterns for Interaction

Tognini (2008) carried out research in French and Italian foreign language classrooms in six Australian secondary schools. Over a four-month period, she observed five lessons in each school, with students aged 14–15 years. Typical of many such classrooms, Tognini found a high proportion of restricted IRF patterns, such as used for drills and reinforcement. For example, a teacher may ask a question (to initiate), the student responds in a predictable way, and the teacher provides some kind of feedback—by repeating what the student said to affirm a correct response, or by indicating an error by recasting it, or asking the student to try again. IRF patterns are generally associated with practice of particular structures or vocabulary. If such practice is contextualized so that it is clearly linked to meaning, it can play a useful role in helping beginner learners to become more automatic in their language use (see Chapter 2).

On the other hand, IRF sequences can limit students to a single turn and this can reduce the actual communicative nature of the interaction. Students might respond by rote—they can give the right answer without necessarily understanding the meaning. However, Tognini also found expanded IRF patterns, and these did provide the opportunity for learners to respond to feedback and modify their first attempts. For example, in Classroom Snapshot 4.4, the teacher of a high school Italian class prompts the learner to try again, giving explicit feedback, and gives the student an opportunity to modify her utterance. Here, as often happens in the classroom, the student is able to 'piggyback' on another student's response.

Classroom Snapshot 4.4

Teacher: … *Ultima domanda. Come si dice* 'Going to the movies'*?* [Last question. How do you say 'Going to the movies'?]

Student 21:   *Ti piace al cinema.* [last work with English pronunciation] [Do you like to the movies?]

Teacher: You're missing a verb. *Ti piace … ?* [You like … ?] [student near the tape says *andare* 'to go']

Student 21:   *Ti piace andare al cinema.* [Do you like to go to the movies?]

(Tognini, 2008, p. 63) ▓

At other times, teacher-led interaction can enable students to take part in a lengthy conversation, as we see in the exchange in Activity 4.3.

Activity 4.3

Look at the teacher's intervention at each arrow point in the teacher–student interaction below. How does each of these interventions help the student maintain the conversation beyond the initial IRF sequence?

1 **Teacher:**   *Come stai oggi, A?* [How are you today, A?]
2 **Student 1:**   *Ho fame.* [I'm hungry.]
3 **Teacher:**   *Ho fame! Non hai mangiato per la colazione?* → [I'm hungry!
                     Didn't you have breakfast?]
4 **Student 1:**   *No.*
5 **Teacher:**   [to someone else in the class] *Occhi a me!* [addressing Student
                    A again] *No? Perchè? Sei troppo contenta del compleanno di
                    ieri? …* [no response from the student] *Sei troppo contenta del
                    compleanno di ieri?* → [Eyes to me! No? Why? Are you too happy
                    about your birthday yesterday? (repeated)]
6 **Student 1:**   What did you say?
7 **Teacher:**   *Sei troppo contenta … del compleanno di ieri? Sei – troppo
                    contenta … del compleanno … di ieri?*
                    [question is repeated very slowly and accompanied by animated
                    non-verbal signals] → [Are you too happy about your birthday
                    yesterday? Are you … too happy … about your birthday …
                    yesterday?]
8 **Student 1:**   *Troppo contenta.* [Too happy.]
9 **Teacher:**   *Si! Ooo … e che cosa mangi per pranzo oggi?* → [Yes! … Ooo …
                    and what are you going to eat for lunch today?]
10 **Student 1:**   Niente. [Nothing.]
11 **Teacher:**   *Niente. Perché? Non hai moneta?* → [Nothing. Why? Don't you
                    have any money?]
12 **Student 1:**   [nods]
13 **Teacher:**   *O poverina!* [Oh you poor thing!]

(Tognini, 2008, cited in Philp & Tognini, 2009, pp. 248–9)

As you can see, the student is carried along in the conversation by the teacher, who modifies her own speech to help the student understand, and asks a series of questions to keep things going (lines 1, 3, 5, 7, 9, 11). In this way, the teacher involves the learner in a conversation that the learner would otherwise struggle to sustain. We noted this kind of scaffolding by the primary school teacher in Classroom Snapshot 3.5, and we can see here that it is also true of high school language classrooms. The rest of the class may also benefit from this interaction between teacher and student as they listen, not just to a rote answer to a predictable question, but to a real and meaningful interaction. Aren't we all most motivated when conversations are relevant to own lives and we get to use language for real purposes?

Purposes for Interaction

Tognini's data were further analyzed and discussed by Tognini and ourselves (Philp & Tognini, 2009; Tognini, Philp, & Oliver, 2010) to look at features of interaction in foreign language classrooms. For example, based on this and other research in primary and secondary foreign language classrooms, Philp & Tognini (2009) suggest three main purposes for interaction in this context: '(1) interaction as practice, including the use of formulaic language; (2) interaction that concentrates on the exchange of information; and (3) collaborative dialogue including attention to form' (p. 254).

With regard to the first purpose, interaction as practice, the three studies we mentioned earlier, from Britain (Mitchell & Martin, 1997), Australia (Tognini, 2008) and New Zealand (Erlam & Sakui, 2006) suggest that teachers often provide restricted language practice, for example, through the use of scripted dialogues, or questions about daily routines. For learners with limited L2 proficiency this practice provides 'time on task' to start to use the target language and to improve accuracy and fluency, through the use of formulaic sequences. In this case, language use is predictable. The benefit to learners is to develop procedural knowledge, so that they gradually become more automatic in language use—like a tennis player learning to swing the racket in the right way by doing it over and over in play until it becomes a natural action (see Chapter 2). For example, in Classroom Snapshot 4.5, where two high school French learners use a series of questions to interview one another on daily routines, Student C repeats the same formulaic expressions, but can substitute different reflexive verbs (and times). This helps them practice the use of these verbs as well as expressions of time. What is important to notice in this case, is that language form matches meaning—Student C reports the time she actually gets up, which (presumably) her partner does not know. DeKeyser (2007) emphasizes the need for such practice to be meaningful (not rote) and thus establish connections between form and meaning.

Classroom Snapshot 4.5

1 **Student D:** *Tu te réveilles à quelle heure?* [At what time do you wake up?]
2 **Student C:** *Je me réveille à sept heures.* [I wake up at seven o'clock.]
3 **Student D:** *A quelle heure tu te lèves?* [At what time do you get up?]
4 **Student C:** *Je me lève à sept heures.* [I get up at seven o'clock.]

(Tognini, Philp, & Oliver, 2010, p. 28.12) ■

In addition to controlled practice like this, which includes some exchange of information, interaction for more extensive communicative purposes is also a feature of many foreign language classrooms, both between the teacher and the whole class and in pair- or group-work. Activities such as information gap tasks, problem-solving, and class surveys (Mitchell & Martin, 1997) can involve students in more creative language use. Such opportunities are essential to oral language development. If learners only engage in controlled practice activities involving use of formulaic phrases, they are unlikely to go beyond this to creative use—that is, to a point where they start to break down formulaic chunks and use them creatively or apply them in a different situation, as seen in Classroom Snapshot 4. 6. Here, the two learners enact a semi-scripted role play between a hotel receptionist and a visitor (obviously from quite an old textbook, since they are using francs not euros to pay!). Student A makes use of the phrase *je voudrais* ('I'd like') a number of times, substituting room and price as needed.

Classroom Snapshot 4.6

1 **Student A:** *Je voudrais une chambre … à une lit et avec une bain … s'il vous plaît. Je voudrais quatre-vingts francs.* [I'd like … a single room with bath … please. I'd like 80 francs.]

2 **Student B:** *No soixante.* (discussion in English indecipherable) [No sixty.]

3 **Student A:** *Je voudrais une chambre … à une grande lit et … une bain … s'il vous plaît. Je voudrais payer … cinquante francs.* [I'd like a room … with a double bed … and bath … please. I'd like to pay … 50 francs.]

(Tognini, 2008, p. 225)

Supporting Successful Language Learning
Formulaic and Creative Language Use

Ellis (2005) suggests that both 'a rich repertoire of formulaic expressions and rule-based competence' are essential for successful instructed language learning. The interactive activities we have noted above can support the acquisition of both. Another way to promote these aspects of language knowledge is through encouraging the use of the target language rather than the L1 by early teaching of common classroom expressions. For example, in Erlam & Sakui's (2006) observation of a French class, they saw the following signs on the walls (without translation): *Je ne suis pas d'accord* ('I don't agree') and *Madame a fait une erreur, oops!* ('The teacher made a mistake, oops!'). In addition, the students had laminated sheets in their folders with expressions (plus translations) that they might need to respond to the teacher about a problem, for example, *Où est mon cahier?* ('Where is my exercise book?'); *Je l'ai laissé dans mon casier* ('I left it in my locker'); *Je l'ai laissé chez moi* ('I left it at home'). In this class, they observed students often using formulaic expressions, such as *Pouvez-vous éteindre la lumière?* ('Can you turn the light off?') and *Il sèche le cours* ('He is skipping class') (p. 12). It is worth pointing out here the motivational benefits of providing learners with age-appropriate models. For example, Tarone & Swain (1995) in research in French immersion classes in Canada, noted adolescents' unwillingness to use the target language in class, in comparison to children in primary school classes. They suggested this reticence was related to issues of identity. The model L2 input in class was primarily from adults—these high school students could speak like teenagers only in their first language. One student reported 'I'd like to be able to sit in a classroom and have someone teach me how to say "Well, come on guys, let's go get some burgers" and stuff like that' (Swain, 1993, pp. 6, 12, cited in Tarone & Swain, 1995, p. 172). Identity and language are closely bound.

There are a number of ways teachers can push learners beyond formulaic use to creative language use. As Ellis (2005) also notes, to develop proficiency, learners need to have the chance to interact in the target language. In foreign language classrooms, particularly in large classes, it can be difficult for learners to have the opportunity to use the target language for real communicative purposes, but authentic language use can be supported in a number of ways. Erlam & Sakui (2006), for example, report that the French teachers in the study encouraged their students to try saying more in French than 'yes' or 'no' responses. They scaffolded this through cuing a response, or providing a choice of responses, as seen in Classroom Snapshot 4.7.

Classroom Snapshot 4.7

Teacher: *Qu'est-ce que nous avons fait aujourd'hui?* [What have we done today?]
Nous avons … [We have …]

Student: *… revisé les phrases.* [… revised the sentences.]

Teacher: *Tu reçois ou tu ne reçois pas d'argent de poche?* [You do or you don't get pocket money?]

Student: *Je reçois.* [I get it.]

(Erlam & Sakui, 2006, p. 16, original formatting not reproduced)

Corrective Feedback

As we have discussed in previous chapters, a feature of teacher-student interaction is the provision of corrective feedback, in the form of recasts, prompts, or explicit correction. There have been a number of studies of corrective feedback in foreign language high school classes (for example, Doughty & Varela, 1998; Lyster & Sato, 2013). What this research has found is that teachers provide a variety of types of feedback and that they are useful in different ways, as we saw in Chapter 2. Studies in high school classes have found recasts to be often the most commonly used, particularly for errors in grammar and pronunciation. Vocabulary problems can be worked through by negotiation or translation, and explicit correction is also common (Nation, 2008).

Peer Interaction in Foreign Language Settings

While high school peer interaction can foster greater autonomy in learning, some teachers prefer to maintain whole class interaction and have misgivings as to the benefits of pair- and group-work (for example, Mitchell & Martin, 1997; Erlam & Sakui, 2007; Tognini, 2008). They are concerned that learners are unable to provide good models, or consistent and accurate feedback to one another. However, research suggests that, when well- managed, peer interaction can make a unique contribution to learning, in ways that complement teacher-led interaction. Among peers, particularly familiar peers and friends, learners can feel less anxious about making mistakes, and may be more willing to try out and experiment with new phrases or structures. This can provide the context learners need to move from formulaic language to generating their own talk. Even if it is non-target like, this is a step towards being able to use target language forms to express themselves. In a review of research on peer interaction, Philp, Adams, & Iwashita (2013) suggested that, in contrast with teacher-led interaction, pair or small group interaction provides more opportunity to try out language, and to build fluency through practice. The risk of making mistakes in a whole class situation can be more of an issue for students in their teens, who can be more self-conscious and inhibited than younger learners. Tognini (2008) makes this point, after interviewing high school students—the activities they enjoyed least were those involving talking in front of the whole class. As we saw in Chapter 2, one student commented:

> *When you're working with your partner, you don't care about being silly …*
> *Like (laughter from other students) when you say the wrong thing, or like*

you try to make up a word of your own that you think is in French and like,
you just have fun with your partner. You don't have to be so serious.

(Tognini, 2008, p. 290)

Hence it would seem that peer interaction also carries with it affective benefits that are motivating for learning—it is fun to work with friends. In Chapter 2, with reference to the work of Swain, we talked about how experimentation and working things out together might be useful for language learning. We also noted the importance of drawing learners' attention to language form in the context of meaningful conversation. In conversation between peers, this tends to be mostly about vocabulary items. Left to their own devices, peers may not provide one another with feedback on grammatical form—maybe they are too shy to, they are not sure how to, or they do not notice the error themselves.

Peers' Attention to Language Form

Working Collaboratively

While oral interaction between students can tend to focus on communication needs rather than on language form, oral tasks that involve some kind of collaborative writing, such as a dictogloss task or a jigsaw task, can do this. Such tasks involve working in pairs or groups to reconstruct a text by pooling the resources of shared notes, and collective knowledge. Discussing how to express a common meaning is particularly conducive to having students try out their language use, and notice problems as they arise. By trial and error, applying their explicit and implicit knowledge to see what seems to fit best, they are pushed in their language output. These are all aspects of the learning process that facilitate learning, as we noted in Chapter 2, and which we see in action in Activity 4.4.

Activity 4.4

Swain & Lapkin (1998) analyzed the oral and written output of two adolescent students, Kim and Rick, in a Grade-8 French immersion class. They were working on a picture jigsaw task. Holding different halves of the story, the two learners had to work out the story together and write it down. Before the task, the class received a short mini lesson on the use of reflexive verbs, and the story elicited use of this form. What effect do you think this could have on their focus as they write the story together?

As you read through this exchange between the two learners, next to each learner's turn, write a short description of what you think each person is doing. Some suggestions are provided for some of the turns.

Rick: *Elle se … et elle se …* how do you say 'follow'? ['She' (reflexive pronoun) … and 'she' (reflexive pronoun)] **Kim:** Hmmm? **Rick:** How do you say 'follow'?	Rick tries to say 'She follows' and intends to make this a reflexive verb, but he doesn't know the right word.
Kim: *Suit.* [Follows.]	Kim
Rick: *Suit. Elle se suit* or *elle suit*? [Follows. 'She follows' (reflexive form) or 'she follows'? (non-reflexive form)]	Rick
Kim: *Elle se … elle LE suive.* [She (reflexive pronoun) … she follows HIM.)	Kim starts to use a reflexive pronoun, but then corrects herself and adds the object pronoun instead. She stresses this addition.
Rick: *Elle le?* [She [follows] him?]	Rick
Kim: *Elle LE suive.* [She follows HIM.]	Kim
Rick: *Jusqu'à l'école.* [To school.]	Rick finishes the sentence.

(Swain & Lapkin, 1998, p. 330, annotations added)

By having to work together, the learners were able to talk through how to express things, although Rick relies on Kim's knowledge to help him out. Here Rick first needs the verb in French, and then starts to think about the form itself, specifically whether the verb requires a reflexive pronoun or not. Kim provides a target like version, emphasizing her addition of the correct object pronoun (*le*). Because the pair have to reconstruct the text and actually write it down, they focus on the details of how to express precisely what they want to say, and to apply their knowledge to help them do this. Interestingly, Rick's answers in pre- and post-tests of his ability to use reflexive pronouns showed that he was mostly correct in his use of this verb form, and that he was reasonably (but not completely) sure of his answers. For him, this interaction was an opportunity to practice applying rules he had studied, but was still unsure. In contrast, Kim was confident and correct in her use of the reflexive verb. This interaction helped her consolidate the knowledge she already had, and to practice applying it, taking a step toward fluent or automatic use of the form.

Such research encourages teachers to see that oral interaction between peers can promote L2 learning by providing opportunities for experimenting with language, practicing forms they know and consolidating their knowledge. It is important to note, however, that Swain & Lapkin found that not all the learners in their study made the effort to concentrate on form as these two did. Clearly, individual differences between learners and how well they work together can make a difference to the outcomes of interaction. For this reason, researchers and educationalists alike emphasize the benefits of training students in effective group-work, as we noted in Chapter 3.

We see another example of outcomes of peers working together in a study by Kuiken & Vedder (2002). They examined the effect of interaction during a dictogloss task on learning of a particular grammatical structure (the passive) by 16–18-year-olds learning English in Holland. In groups of three or four, the high school learners carried out two dictogloss tasks together. Each text contained many passives of varying complexity, for example, 'it was owned', 'it had been stolen', 'it should have been given'. They found that peer interaction on these reconstruction tasks fostered noticing and discussion of language form, as seen in Classroom Snapshot 4.8. You will see in this example that the students used Dutch to support their L2 production. Metalinguistic talk (for example, 'you're not allowed to put "it" at the end'; 'past tense, passive') occurred mostly in Dutch (translated below in italics), while they used English to try out different possibilities.

Classroom Snapshot 4.8

Boris: Her ancestors were given it.

Tom: Were given it?

Boris: *Yes that should be the right form.*

Tom: *Yes but … I think … You cannot say it that way in English.*

Boris: *Why not? Past tense, passive.*

Tom: But it … It *shouldn't stand all the way at the end.*

Boris: *Oh that's what you mean, so* It was given toy.

Tom: *Yeah that's it because* her ancestors were given it … *I think you're not allowed to put* it *at the end that's not possible sounds wrong so* It was … it was given to her ancestors.

(Kuiken & Vedder, 2002, p. 356, original formatting not reproduced) ■

You can see that in their discussion the students use both their implicit knowledge ('it sounds wrong') and their metalinguistic knowledge to help them out ('Why not? Past tense, passive'). Philp, Adams, & Iwashita (2013) note that writing can help to anchor language form. For example, the visual input of this dictogloss task (i.e. the writing) may have helped make certain features of language more salient for learners. In this way, oral and written work can complement and assist each other.

Classroom Snapshot 4.8 illustrates an important feature of peer interaction: it provides the opportunity for learners to test out hypotheses about how to say things in the target language—whether right or wrong—and to draw attention to the problems, a crucial step in language development (see Chapter 2). In this way, it can complement whole class interaction through deepening learners' engagement with language and orienting them to the form if it appears in teacher talk or other input (written or aural). For example, in Classroom Snapshot 4.8, although Tom's hypothesis in the last line may be incorrect, the discussion serves to highlight the problem, and may lead the students to notice examples of the form in other input in later lessons. This is a central feature of Spotlight Study 4.3.

Spotlight Study 4.3

Toth, Wagner, & Moranksi (2013) looked at high school learners' ability to formulate explicit grammar rules based on seeing examples of a particular form in written texts. They looked at Spanish lessons in a US high school class. This class comprised 17 students, aged 15–18 years (13 males and four females) and a female teacher who was a non-native speaker of Spanish. The study reflects the ability of adolescents to talk about language in a decontextualized way, and to recognize underlying patterns in another language that may be different to those in their first language. In each written text the students saw the target form (the reflexive form *se* in Spanish) used in diverse ways. In small groups they had to work out how and why *se* was used differently—that is, to connect form and meaning. They achieved this by a combination of group-work, where they worked inductively to try to sort out the different ways *se* was used, and teacher–student interaction, in which the teacher guided them with questions to resolve difficulties. This way of learning was a new experience for these learners, who normally received more explicit deductive grammar explanations in English. The target structure is usually problematic for English-speaking learners because its use matches different forms in English: the passive (for example, **Se** *lavaron los suéteres*, 'The sweaters were washed'); transitivity/non-agency (for example, *Los suéteres* **se** *secaron*, 'The sweaters [Ø] dried', i.e someone dried the sweaters); reflexive (for example, *Los niños* **se** *secaron*, 'The children dried themselves/each other') (Toth et al., 2013, p. 294, original formatting not reproduced).

Over three lessons, the students were given reading texts which each time highlighted a different function of the use of *se* (for example, a newspaper article about a Chilean earthquake). They worked on the meaning of the text, and then identified uses of the target structure. Working in small groups they had to come up with rules to explain differences in the uses of *se*. This was followed by a teacher-led whole class discussion of their suggested rules in English. They then applied the rules in communicative use of *se*. In the following peer group discussion, the two partners collaboratively work out the rule, which Jose articulates in (d). In these examples, Toth et al. highlight reference to meaning by italics, and reference to form by bold type. In many cases, both apply—the learners are thinking through connections between form and meaning.

(a) **Alberto:** If the **direct object** *is itself* you would use= **you would use se**

(b) **Jose:** Well it's, eh, like the same thing as last time. When **the verb** is eh **defined** or like it's … ah what's the word … I'm drawin' a blank here Alberto … *specified* there we go.

(c) **Alberto:** Eh yeah.

(d) **Jose:** When **the verb** is *specified* it **follows the verb** but *when it's not* it like **follows the direct object** again.

(e) **Alberto:** Sounds good.

(Toth et al., 2013, p. 293, original formatting not reproduced)

Another group also focuses on the direct object as a clue to understanding the use of *se*, this time to describe the use of the passive in the context of a recipe. Pepe focuses on contrasting two sentences and notes patterns in what he sees, but he does not yet articulate a rule.

(a) **Pepe:** Anyway so I said this before but the only thing that **seems to change** is um the second column. It's *in general* and **the subject conjugation** um **refers to the direct object** um because like=

(b) **Jesús:** Because you're not smart enough=

(c) **Pepe:** =It changes to um like *the general form* for like … from **Graciela pela los chiles** [Graciela peels the peppers] … well it's **pela los chiles** because it's saying *Graciela is the subject* so obviously it would be conjugated in the **third person singular** form. But then for the *recipes the general* it's **se pelan los chiles** [The chillies are peeled] and the only thing that changed is that um the **direct object is plural**. So that it became **pelan** and not the singular **pela** … [continues with other examples that follow the same pattern]

(d) **Luis:** What?

(e) **Jesús:** Ca= can you repeat that again?

(Toth et al., 2013, p. 293, original formatting not reproduced)

Pepe's partners, Luis and Jesús, add little, but in a later response to the teacher about verb agreement, Jesús actually repeats Pepe's agreement rule in his own words: 'So basically the verb's in like he, she, you, *Usted* form kinda thing, if it's –like the direct object over here – is singular'. This suggests that he was taking in what Pepe said, although at the time he seemed nonplussed.

Toth et al. found that the learners were able to categorize the uses of *se* that they saw, correctly identify patterns of use, and formulate rules to a limited extent. However, the learners varied greatly in how well they managed this, and some participated much more than others. In the classroom discussion that followed, the teacher helped to extend their understanding, initially by drawing their attention to distinctive and contrasting characteristics of the sentences, and this appeared to help them formulate rules more clearly. Pepe, for example, develops his ideas more clearly and is able to articulate a working hypothesis or rule about the use of *se* in the earthquake text. We see that initially the students struggle to explain the absence of *se* to express the idea that heavy rain soaked the people (the verb *mojar*, 'to wet', is used transitively without se), but then Pepe finds a way to explain it. Although this is not initially understood by all, it is helpful to some.

(a) **T:** What's going on with **the doer of the verb** in this first column **frases sin se** [sentences without *se*]? Who's **the doer** of that **of those actions**?

(b) **Lucas:** Um well it's usually **a person**.

(c) **T:** Uh huh.

(d) **Lucas:** **Except for the llu= la lluvia**. [heavy rain]

(e) **T:** Uh huh. OK.

(f) **Lucas:** And **it does something to something else**.

(g) **T:** OK. And but then that's in comparison to the other column right? What's going on in the other column with the verbs *sin=* **the verbs that have se**?

(h) **Pepe:** Um even though technically you could say that **what did it is the tornado** in all cases it we're just looking to find **subject** and **verbs**. We're saying that the thing that the **doer is** like **the thing it happened to**. So like the wind= **las ventanas se abieron=** so like **the windows opened**. It's **the windows that opened** like they didn't do it **of their own volition** but that still what we're saying **the windows opened**.

(i) **T:** What di= does that make sense to you guys?

(Toth et al., 2013, pp. 295–6, original formatting not reproduced)

This illustrates that students' can go some way to understanding grammar in an inductive way when they talk about it together, although there are some limitations. One person can dominate, or be left to do the work and this could result in a lack of engagement among some other learners in the group

(O'Donnell, 2006). The researchers note that in peer work, the students tended to give up quickly when analysis became difficult, and 'engaged in unrelated topics rather than exploring possible alternatives' (p. 296). However, this does not reflect the whole story—the potential of peer work must be understood in combination with the whole lesson, because it plays a complementary role to teacher-led interaction (Philp, Adams, & Iwashita, 2013; Batstone & Philp, 2013). Would Pepe have arrived at his conclusion if he had not talked it through with his peers first? It was during interaction with the teacher that the students managed greater and more in-depth analytic talk. In this context, the teacher tended to categorize while the students engaged in more identification of patterns and rule formation.

Toth et al. suggest that the fact that learners worked on the rule inductively together first helped them engage with language at a deeper level and make use of the scaffolding by the teacher. Swain & Lapkin (2001) similarly talk about 'languaging' in this way (see also Chapter 2). Toth et al., also emphasize the importance of training students in productive collaboration and discussion, as we noted earlier in the chapter. ▉

Strengths and Limitations

Spotlight Study 4.3 reflects particular strengths of high school students as language learners—they are able to engage in abstract and theoretical discussion, albeit not always using accurate terminology, and they can make use of inductive reasoning and explicit rules to support their language learning. It is also interesting to see here the use of L1 to facilitate discussion of form and meaning of the target language. Inductive teaching techniques may particularly suit certain learners and may pose greater difficulty for others according to individual differences. This is discussed in the following section.

Individual Differences

Learners differ according to their past knowledge and experience in language and content learning. They also differ in their aptitude for language learning, their motivation to learn, and preferences for how they best learn. We will now explore what this might mean for a learner's potential to get the most out of certain classroom activities.

Aptitude

As we discussed in Chapter 2, individual differences can make an impact on language learning, with some adolescents more advantaged than others in some learning or testing situations. For example, with regard to language aptitude, researchers have found that some kinds of instruction can favor certain abilities such as a strength in working memory, memory for sounds, mimicry, or language analytic ability.

In a study carried out in three French high school classes in New Zealand, Erlam (2003) taught three classes with students aged 14–15 years in their second year of learning French. She used a different way of teaching grammar for each class over three sessions. In one class, the students were taught in a **deductive** way, that is, the teacher provided explicit explanation of the rules behind the target language form (indirect object pronouns), and required students to produce the target structures. In another class, the students were taught in an **inductive** way—they carried out practice activities with a focus on comprehension and production, and had to explain their choices. In this way, they did not discuss rules, but they did have to make connections between form and meaning to complete the task. A third class received **structured input**—they had lots of input-based activities that encouraged them to focus on form and meaning, but didn't require any production. All students completed pre-tests before the instruction, and then post-tests and delayed post-tests after instruction, which tested oral and written production, as well as reading and listening comprehension. The potential advantage of aptitude varied according to type of instruction and task. Erlam found that in these teacher-centered classes, a deductive approach was most effective, and that for the deductive group, aptitude didn't make a difference to how well they did on tests (although it did for the other groups). This suggests that this type of instruction was of benefit to all learners for learning this particular form. Overall, it was students with higher analytic ability who gained the most on written production tests regardless of instruction type. That is, the ability to see patterns in language (language analytic ability) was of greatest benefit to students on the written production tasks, but this ability wasn't so important for oral production. From this study we see that strengths in language aptitude are more crucial in some learning contexts and types of tasks than others.

Motivation

In Chapter 2, we also emphasized the importance of motivation in learning. This includes how hard students are willing to work at something, but also how long they are going to pursue it. Adolescents' attitudes are also part of this—including their attitudes towards the language, and the people who speak it, as well as to language learning in general, and their reasons for learning a particular language (and whether they have a choice about it).

Activity 4.5

In a study conducted in Budapest, Hungary, Kormos & Csìzer (2008) compared the motivations for language learning among high school students, university students, and adults. Like other motivation researchers, they investigated different aspects of motivation. Look at Tables 4.2 and 4.3 below, which provide a selection of factors related to motivation, and sample questions asked in the questionnaire. Students were asked to fill out a questionnaire indicating how much they agreed (Table 4.2) or how much it was true of them (Table 4.3). Which factors do you think were most important to high school students as an influence on their motivation for learning English? Put a check next to those you think might most motivate learners at this age (whether positively or negatively).

Factor	Description	Example of a question	Check
Integrativeness	Learners' attitude to L2 speakers and their cultures	How much would you like to become similar to the people who speak English?	
Cultural interest	Attitudes to L2 cultural products (films, TV programs, magazines, pop culture)	How much do you like the films made in the USA?	

Photocopiable © Oxford University Press

Table 4.2 Factors influencing motivation: agreement

Factor	Description	Example of a question	Check
Language use anxiety	The level of anxiety felt when students use English everyday life	I would feel uneasy speaking English with a native speaker.	
Classroom anxiety	The level of anxiety felt in language classes	It embarrasses me to volunteer answers in our English class.	
Milieu	The attitude of people in the students' immediate environment concerning the importance of learning English	People around me tend to think it is a good thing to know foreign languages.	
Parental encouragement	The extent to which parents encourage their children to study English	My parents really encourage me to study English.	

Factor	Description	Example of a question	Check
Language learning attitudes	The extent to which students like learning English	I really enjoy learning English.	
Ideal L2 self	Students' views of themselves as successful L2 speakers	I like to think of myself as someone who will be able to speak English.	
Motivated learning behavior	Students' efforts and persistence in learning English	I am willing to work hard at learning English.	

Photocopiable © Oxford University Press

Table 4.3 Factors influencing motivation: in relation to self (adapted from Kormos & Csìzer, 2008, pp. 335–6)

Interestingly, there were distinct age differences. The high school students (202 in number) were on average 16.5 years old and in their second or third year of learning English. Their responses showed that they were most influenced by their teachers and by their classroom experience, including enjoyment, in their attitudes to language learning. In contrast, older students had clearer goals for themselves that were less dependent on teacher or classroom experience—they could picture themselves as being competent speakers of the language in the long term (Dörnyei, 2005, calls this their 'ideal L2 self'). This difference reflects adolescents emerging identity and self-image—their idea of themselves is still under construction. For these learners, the encouragement of their parents, and parents' attitudes to language learning was influential. This was also found to be true of UK high school learners of French in a study by Williams & Burden (1997). In interviews with school students in years 6 (primary school), 7, 9, and 10, they found that the older learners (years 9 and 10) tended to judge their ability in language learning by what the teachers wrote in reports and assignments, and by their results. In contrast, younger children gauged success by what they could do.

What are the implications of such studies on motivation? You will see descriptions of integrativeness, milieu, and cultural interest in Table 4.1. These three were found to be the key factors in high school students' motivation. They all relate to learners' perception and attitudes towards the L2 speakers and culture. Many teachers provide opportunities for their students to use authentic materials related to popular culture (for example, music lyrics from popular bands; cartoons on TV and the internet; social media sites; and online interviews with movie stars), and set up possibilities to engage with L2 speakers of their age (for example, pen pals, online chat sessions with students at an overseas school). The study of Kormos & Csìzer (2008) suggests that these are productive ways of motivating their students in language learning, not just for the activity itself, but for the longer term. Another finding was that, compared to older learners, high school learners tended to be less willing than adult learners to invest effort and to persist in language learning—this suggests high school teachers have a greater challenge in helping learners sustain motivation to work at language learning and continue in this. Kormos & Csìzer also found that anxiety in L2 interactions in the classroom, although not high in general, was a problem for about ten percent of all students regardless of age. Dörnyei encourages teachers to be proactive in creating a safe learning climate where students respect one another's efforts, and can try out things without fear of ridicule. Cohesiveness within groups and a good student–teacher relationship are also important steps towards countering the reluctance of older children and adolescents to try using the L2 in interaction with others (Dörnyei 2001a; Dörnyei & Maldarez, 1997).

Summary

Adolescents face many challenges over the high school years. It is a time of tremendous change cognitively, emotionally, physically, and socially. These changes also impact on the nature of oral interaction and processes of learning. Adolescents' increasing autonomy and superior cognitive abilities suggest a greater potential to learn independently in class and through collaborative work with peers. However, scaffolding by the teacher is often necessary to stretch them further in difficult tasks. We also saw that print literacy can support oral literacy and vice versa, particularly with complex texts and tasks, which can often be outside learners' everyday experience. Rather than a hindrance, L1 can support L2 production.

In foreign language settings, where there is less L2 input and less opportunity to use the target language compared to L2 mainstream classes, instructional practices which include a focus on language form are particularly important. This draws learners' attention to elements of language not noticed incidentally. With regard to this, we have emphasized that high school learners can take advantage of their analytic skills and ability to identify and articulate patterns in language to support their oral production. We also saw that peer interaction complements teacher-led interaction. Teacher–student interaction can provide scaffolding of language production, corrective feedback as well as feedback on comprehension of content. Practice activities between learners can then provide a platform for learners to proceduralize their knowledge, providing vital 'time on task'. Collaborative pair- and group-work offers a context for developing confidence in using unfamiliar language, experimenting with form and meaning, and making use of formulaic sequences in new contexts.

It is also important to remember the role of individual differences in language learning in secondary school contexts. The significance of individual difference factors such as aptitude or learning style varies according to context; sometimes they matter more than other times—students can be advantaged or disadvantaged depending on the type of instruction or task. Mindful of individual differences among their students, teachers may consciously vary their way of teaching so as to provide different kinds of learning experiences. This appears to be a good strategy to ensure all students have the chance to make the most of their own strengths and be supported in areas they find difficult. Varying between teacher-led interaction, individual, pair-work, and group-work is an important way of catering for different needs.

5

Oral Interaction: What We Know Now

Preview

In this chapter, we will return to the statements about oral interaction that you responded to in Activity 1.1. For each statement, we will provide a response in light of the information presented in this book. Before you read the responses, review your own ideas by returning to your responses in Activity 1.1.

Activity 5.1 Review your opinions
In Activity 1.1 (page 4), you indicated how strongly you agreed with some statements about oral interaction. Before you continue reading this chapter, go back and complete the questionnaire again. Compare the responses you gave then to those you would give now. Have your views about oral interaction been changed or confirmed by what you have read in the preceding chapters?

Reflecting on Ideas about Oral Interaction

1 Language learners don't need to be taught how to speak as they pick it up in the classroom. It is more important to focus on reading and writing.

Oral interaction is distinct from written language and teaching it is just as important as teaching reading and writing. While it's true that children, particularly younger children, will pick up language as they observe and participate in classroom activities, research tells us that they also benefit from opportunities to interact with others as this facilitates their second language learning. Along with both formal and informal interaction, children also require teachers' explicit instruction, particularly about language associated with formal schooling and more academic content areas. Further, because students come from a variety of backgrounds, some vastly different from the school context they find themselves in, providing opportunities for interaction is integral to their being socialized into local classroom practices. This includes helping them to become familiar with the different types of talk that occur in the classroom, and to follow the different rules about who can speak, when, how, and about what.

In addition, there is much that we can do in our classrooms to help second language learners as they move along their interlanguage continuum. Although interaction is collaborative and can be co-constructed with other learners, there may be times when teachers need to intervene, for example, to provide feedback on non-target like language use, or to scaffold language production, and, at the very least, to create opportunities that promote interaction. This may be particularly important as students move through the grades of their schooling and the topics that are discussed become more complex and abstract.

We must also remember that unlike the first language situation, for learners acquiring their second language, reading and writing are learned at the same time as listening and speaking. It is important to be aware that for second language learners, oral interaction supports not only content and curriculum learning, but also language and literacy development, including learning to read and write.

2 *Oral interaction activities are most useful for helping learners practice language they already know.*

In fact, we argue that people learn language by using language, not just the language they know, but also the language they need to learn (Hatch, 1983). Whilst practicing language is important to proceduralize existing knowledge—to put it into practice and work towards becoming more fluent—interaction also provides opportunities to foster those conditions that facilitate second language acquisition. As Nation (2007) describes, teachers need to provide learners with the opportunity for meaning-focused input, meaning-focused output, language-focused learning, as well as practice leading to fluency development. Each of these components can be provided through oral interaction, and they each support different aspects of language learning.

3 *It is too hard for students to use the target language in the classroom all the time.*

It is certainly difficult. The effort that is required to use a new language can be exhausting for learners. Teachers, too, can find it hard to convey information to students whose language ability is limited. Behavioral problems can also present difficulties. We have argued that first language use can have a role in a second language learning context. At the same time, current research supports a language teaching context in which meaningful target language use is encouraged and supported. Lower proficiency learners can be supported in their language production through the use of formulaic sequences, and by scaffolded conversation with the teacher. In this way, language learners have access to meaningful input that aids comprehension. Further, there is also the chance for learners to practice the target language and by doing so, develop fluency and automaticity.

4 It is more useful for students to practice speaking with the teacher in the whole class than with each other in groups.

In the early stages of learning a language, there is no doubt that teachers provide essential L2 input to the class and also provide models for language use. In addition, teachers' scaffolding of student production can be a first step towards independent L2 practice. Also, teachers are a reliable source of feedback—correcting errors, filling in for missing knowledge, and drawing attention to key forms. However, relying on teacher-led interactions with the whole class means far less time for each individual to try out language, if only because of the number of others involved in the discourse. Teachers have a great deal of control over turn-taking and the content of the talk. In whole-class activities, the needs and interests of individual learners may be overlooked. Therefore, interaction with peers complements the contributions of teachers in important ways and so we would suggest it is useful not to think of it as an 'either/or' choice. Peers, like teachers, are a valuable language learning resource. Having to work out problems in expressing themselves encourages learners to engage more deeply with language form, meaning, and use, and it promotes greater autonomy in learning.

Peers can also contribute to learners' academic, social, and cultural success. Providing opportunities to work with peers builds upon the social nature of interaction and enables learners to build relationships and to develop social affiliation—aspects that are particularly vital to children and adolescent learners' sense of self and well-being. In turn, this can make language learning fun and motivating. Thus, providing students with the chance to engage in collaborative interaction with each other is just as important as practicing speaking in whole-class activities, though they may not be as accurate or seemingly as efficient!

5 Speaking the target language with other students in pairs and groups just reinforces mistakes.

In fact, peer interaction can be a rich and valuable resource for language learners. Peers can provide each other with elements of interaction that support language learning—such as comprehensible input and output, and feedback about attempts. Teachers, however, may be concerned with the potential inaccuracy and inconsistency of peer feedback. Certainly, peer feedback alone is not sufficient for all learners' needs in terms of correction and guidance. However, peers can help one another to recognize problems in their language and to start to think about how to reformulate language—a crucial first step towards change. Like teachers, peers can also provide scaffolding to each other that can support their second language learning. Further, learners can work at their own level—for some this may mean simply using formulaic language to complete tasks, for others, collaborative discourse and 'languaging' can enable learners to move themselves along their own interlanguage continuum.

6 Speaking the target language can be fun and motivating, but students learn more by writing and reading, or studying grammar.

In many classrooms, it would seem that teachers' actions are based on this belief because there is less focused instruction on how to engage in oral interaction than there is on other skills. Yet we have argued that oral interaction provides learners with a model for language learning and a context in which to use both the language they know and the language features they are learning. By interacting with others, learners will be supported both to use and learn the language. At the same time, speaking the target language can be fun and motivating, and as teachers we need to provide ample opportunities for students to do this.

7 Scripted role-play is the most useful speaking practice because students use the target language correctly without mistakes.

Whilst scripted language, such as written role-plays, can provide valuable practice, it needs to be complemented by opportunities for learners to make meaning for themselves. Learners need to have the opportunity to express themselves and engage with how to put language forms together to make sense. When learners attempt to create their own meaningful output in this way, language learning is facilitated. In addition, interactions that involve spontaneous language use and that are meaningful to the speakers promote the occurrence of discourse strategies that help them to negotiate for meaning, make sense of new language, and draw attention to language form.

In turn, these strategies provide learners with a second look at the input. They help make meaning clearer, and also support learners' vocabulary and phonological development. When interacting, learners receive feedback (be this implicit or explicit, or in the form of metalinguistic comment) on their attempts and this is helpful as it enables learners to notice problems in their own production.

8 Pair-work and group-work interaction between learners is useful because it is motivating and less stressful than whole class interaction.
Providing opportunities for peers to work together responds to the developmental interests and needs of children and adolescents. Peer interaction is a useful pedagogical tool because of the social opportunities and enjoyment it can provide (for example, through language play). At its best, students find working with others in pairs or groups motivating and less stressful than whole-class interaction. It is a space in which they can try out new language. Practicing with friends also means they are less worried about making mistakes, and are more likely to take risks. This can help learners move from formulaic production to more creative language use.

At worst, such pair- and group-work can involve unequal participation. One learner may dominate others and/or some learners may sit back 'loafing' cognitively or socially, and rely on others to do the work. This highlights the need for teachers to prepare learners for pair- and group-work: ensuring they all understand the task, have something they need to contribute in order for the task to be completed, and that they have the language and background knowledge required by the task. It also suggests the importance of training learners in how to collaborate effectively, including how to listen to one another, and encourage equal participation.

9 It is just as important to develop students' social speaking skills as it is to develop their oral language for academic purposes.
Oral interaction serves linguistic, academic, and social functions and whilst in language classrooms we tend to focus on the linguistic and academic, there is no doubt that there is also a need to help learners acquire the social functions as well. For example, there may be a need to teach explicitly how to interact appropriately within oral interaction discourse—particularly how the rules of social propriety will alter according to audience and context.

However, we also know that language for social purposes develops more rapidly than does the type of language necessary for academic discourse. Whilst both are important, the proficiency that learners have may vary at any point in time. Learners may be proficient with BICS, but not with CALP until much later. It is vital for teachers to be aware of this and provide language learners the opportunity to develop both.

10 Context makes all the difference to how we say things.
Part of our communicative ability is adjusting the way we say things according to our audience, topic, setting, and context. It is for this reason that we must provide learners with a variety of contexts in which to interact, from the social to the academic.

Context is also important because of the dynamic relationship between language and culture, and how this is embedded in the school curriculum. As teachers there is much we can do to support language learners (for example, scaffolding and providing opportunities for language use in supportive classroom environments).

Conclusion

In this book, we have covered a wide span of age and development, from the first to the last years of school. We have seen that these learners of various ages have particular strengths for language learning. Regardless of whether learners are in primary or secondary school, we have seen that oral interaction plays a vital role in language learning. At the same time, we acknowledged that individual differences can affect language learning outcomes. For example, differences in language aptitude, particularly in working memory or in learning style and personality, can advantage one student over another in particular environments, regardless of age or background.

In concluding our discussion of oral interaction in primary and secondary language classrooms, it is useful to recall Nation's four components of language learning and teaching discussed in Chapter 2. We can see that different elements can fulfill these four needs. The teacher's interaction with the class provides valuable meaning-focused input. This input is made comprehensible to the learner through the shared context of the class—familiar routines help learners to guess what is being talked about, and to pick up repeated formulaic phrases. Gesture, facial expression, and visual aids also assist in this, in addition to a shared L1. Opportunities for meaning-focused output are provided by scaffolded conversations with the teacher, as well as some pair- and group-work tasks, especially when they encourage creative use of language. Language production can be supported by formulaic phrases, particularly in the early stages. More experimental use of language and the opportunity to try out language in different contexts allows learners to start to break down these formulaic phrases and use them productively for a range of meanings. For younger children, pretend play (for example, pretending to be someone else) can be particularly conducive to the development of different ways to express meaning. Language-focused learning, in which learners deliberately pay attention to language features that they need in the context of meaningful communication, can occur through both peer interaction and teacher-led interaction. These two interactional contexts can play complementary roles. We also noted that in peer interaction, learners' attention should be deliberately oriented in some way, for example, through the task itself (as in a collaborative task that involves the learners creating or reconstructing a text together), or by explicit instruction from the teacher (for example, to identify and explain differences in language form or language use). Older school-aged learners have the capacity to think and talk about language form in a decontextualized way and recognize patterns in language, and such metalinguistic thinking can support language learning. Finally, fluency development is supported by the use of controlled practice activities when form is linked to meaning and when language is both predictable and involves an exchange of meaning. This helps learners to proceduralize their knowledge, get used to saying things in a certain way, and to make specific connections between form and meaning.

Because it is so much a part of classroom life, oral interaction can go largely unnoticed. It is often assumed that the difficulty that learners experience in interacting with others is something that will resolve itself over time. Similarly the interrelationship between oral and print literacy development is often not given sufficient consideration. We hope that this book encourages you to make the most of teacher–student and peer interaction, and picture the possibilities for your students.

Suggestions for Further Reading

There are a number of publications about the contribution of interaction to second language acquisition. Below we list nine items that you may find useful. Not all are specific to school age learners, but all provide valuable background for understanding classroom interaction for learning language and using language to learn other subjects in school.

Dörnyei, Z. & Murphey, T. (2003). *Group dynamics in the language classroom.* Cambridge: Cambridge University Press.

Group dynamics is something we could not cover in this book, but it is very important to interaction. While not specific to school contexts, Dörnyei and Murphey's book provides a better understanding of what is behind good classroom dynamics, including group development, group norms, student roles, leadership functions, and conflict management.

Gibbons, P. (2006). *Bridging discourses in the ESL classroom: Students, teachers and researchers.* London: Continuum.

Strongly influenced by the work of Vygotsky and Halliday, Gibbons' book explores the interactions that take place in two upper primary classrooms, between the teachers and students, and between the students themselves. Packed with everyday examples from these two classes, this is an illuminating study of how interaction can support not only second language learning, but also the development of curriculum knowledge.

Lightbown, P. & Spada, N. (2013). *How languages are learned 4e.* Oxford: Oxford University Press.

A very accessible and understandable explanation of how languages are learned. In addition to explaining theory with sound research, it also provides real and engaging examples. Unlike other SLA texts, many of the examples are from child learners, often working in second language classrooms.

Mackey, A. & Polio, C. (Eds). (2009). *Multiple perspectives on interaction: Second language research in honor of Susan. M. Gass.* New York, NY: Routledge.

This book provides a collection of recent reports of research on interaction and second language learning. Although the majority of studies here involve adult learners, they address many of the issues we have discussed in relation to children, and the book features work by world-renowned experts in the field including Swain, Spada, and Lightbown.

Mercer, N. & Hodgkinson, S. (Eds). (2008). *Exploring talk in school.* London: Sage Publications.

This is a collection of readings about interaction in mainstream classrooms. Although it does not talk about second language learners, it is very useful for understanding the many roles of oral production in schools and how to improve the use we make of classroom talk for learning, thinking, exploring, evaluating, and for managing social relations. Some of the important concepts that we have discussed in this volume are based on the work done by the authors whose work appears in this book, for example, the role of exploratory talk, teachers' use of feedback, and the relationship between 'talking to learn and learning to talk' in academic subject matter classes.

Nation, I. S. P. & Newton, J. (2009). *Teaching ESL/EFL listening and speaking.* London: Taylor & Francis.

This is a very readable and practical book about teaching listening and speaking. Although not specific to secondary and primary school contexts, many of the principles and ideas are appropriate, and highlight the important role of oral interaction in learning.

Philp, J., Adams, R., & Iwashita, N. (2013). *Peer interaction and second language learning.* New York: Taylor & Francis.

This book discusses what research on instructed language learning has to say about peer interaction in the classroom, its potential benefits, and limitations for language learning. It includes two chapters specific to second language learners in schools—one explores differences according to age; the other explores the social nature of peer interaction.

Philp, J., Oliver, R., & Mackey, A. (Eds). (2008). *Child's play? Second language acquisition and the younger learner*. Amsterdam: John Benjamins.

This collection of work focuses on the distinct nature of child second language learning. There are 16 chapters, including a comprehensive introduction, exploring how the cognitive, emotional, and social development of children and adolescents affects their second language learning. The various chapters raise important questions about the implications for pedagogy of the unique characteristics of younger learners.

Toohey, K. (2000). *Learning English in school: Identity, social relations and classroom practice*. Clevedon: Multilingual Matters.

This book presents the stories of three years of observation of classes in a Canadian school among children of mixed culture and languages, following their progress in second language English use from kindergarten to Grade 2. It provides valuable insights into the language learning experiences of the children, their peers, and their teachers in such settings.

Glossary

automaticity: the ability to do something without having to think consciously about it. This develops through practice and repetition.

BICS (Basic Interpersonal Communication Skills): the language skills required for conversational fluency in everyday face to face contextualized communication (Cummins, 1981).

CALP (Cognitive Academic Language Proficiency): the linguistic ability needed to use language in academic, decontextualized contexts (for example, reading) (Cummins, 1981).

child-directed speech: the language (formerly called 'Motherese') that caregivers use when interacting with babies and young children. It has a particular pattern and includes the use of simplified vocabulary, particular intonation contours, repetition, questioning, deixis (pointing), and a slower rate of speech.

collaborative, collaboration: working together in cooperative ways, learning socially, and involving a joint construction of meaning and understanding.

comprehensible output: a term used by Swain (1985, 1985) to describe a learner's attempt to say or write something in a second language in a way that will make sense.

comprehensible output hypothesis: the hypothesis of Swain (1985, 1995) that the act of producing language in either oral or written form contributes to the process of second language learning, particularly when learners are pushed to express themselves in ways that are both coherent in terms of content and accurate in terms of form.

declarative knowledge: the knowledge of the language system one is able to articulate explicitly, such as the meaning of a word, or the reason for the use of a particular grammatical form, for example, rules such as 'Third person verbs in the simple present end in -s'.

decoding: understanding the representation of meaning in a language either in sound (when someone speaks) or symbol (writing on a page). In English, the ability to decode writing is based on knowledge of letter–sound relationships.

deductive: a learning situation in which explicit rules or explanations are given about a particular language form before it is practiced. In contrast, see 'inductive'.

deictic; deixis: referring to words that function to specify or point to something we are talking or writing about, such as 'there', 'that', 'this', 'it'.

dictogloss: an activity that is designed to help learners focus on the form of language while they work together in pairs or groups to express a given meaning in writing. Teachers prepare a text containing the desired language forms. This is read to the class while they take notes. Students then work collaboratively in groups to reconstruct the text that is accurate in terms of meaning and form.

disfluency/-ies: referring to breaks in the flow of speech, such as pauses, hesitation, repetition, false starts, for example, 'I um ah wan= wanted to um add one th thing'.

ellipsis: the omission of part of a sentence that is already understood from the context or from a previous utterance, and there for doesn't need to be fully stated (for example, 'Coming?' is an incomplete sentence; 'Are you?' is ellipted, as the meaning 'Are you coming?' is assumed). Ellipsis is a common feature of oral interaction.

encoding: the process of storing meaning in memory. Encoding can also refer to making meaning through the use of symbols, such as by writing.

exploratory talk: the type of classroom talk learners use in the early stages of developing their thoughts and ideas. It may be 'hesitant and incomplete' as learners try out new ideas, and sort information into different patterns (Barnes 2008, p. 5). In contrast, see 'presentational talk'.

fluency development: learners' growing ability to become more adept at producing language more quickly in 'real' time, without numerous hesitations or long pauses. It develops through practice and repetition.

foreign language: a language not used in the community in which it is being learned (for example, French in Australia, Japanese in Canada).

form focus: (also described as 'focus on form') it entails instruction in which learners are made aware of the form (for example, grammar, lexis, phonology, morphology, etc.) within a communicative use of language.

formulaic language: a fixed pattern of words that are stored and retrieved from memory as a whole rather than as separate components. For example, greetings and routine questions and answers such as 'How are you today?' as well as units such as 'once upon a time' or 'in other words'.

inductive: in relation to language learning, learners work out (induce) the rule or pattern underlying language forms from examples gleaned from experience or provided in classroom input. In contrast, see 'deductive'.

information processing: a model of learning that likens the brain to a computer, with the ability to process and store information. Active processing requires attention, and attentional resources are limited and restrict how much a person is able to process at any one time. Being able to rely on automatic processing (i.e. without conscious attention) is crucial. The more we process automatically (without conscious attention), the more attention we have for other things.

input hypothesis: the hypothesis of Krashen (1977) that, when language input is comprehensible, second language learning will occur. The input must also include language that is just beyond the learner's current stage of development (i.e. the 'i + 1 principle', where i = interlanguage, and +1 is a little more).

interaction hypothesis: the hypothesis of Long (1983, modified 1996) that for acquisition to occur, learners must engage in meaningful interaction that reflects a need for mutual comprehensibility.

interaction for academic purposes: using language in meaningful ways with others to talk about topics that are academic rather than social in orientation, for example, to talk about content in subject areas such as mathematics, science, and history.

interaction for social purposes: using language in meaningful ways with others to talk about topics that are social rather than academic in orientation.

interlanguage/interlanguage continuum: the systematic 'grammar' of a learner's language that can feature elements of both the L1 and the L2, as well as elements found in neither. It follows a pattern of changes that occur from zero proficiency to target like proficiency in the second language (Selinker, 1972).

IRF pattern (initiation-response-feedback): a three-turn pattern of interaction between a teacher and students, especially in whole-class activities. It involves: (1) the teacher initiating the sequence, often with a question; (2) the student responding; and (3) the teacher replying with positive or negative feedback. Such a pattern of exchange has been criticized for being teacher-centred and not focused on real communication.

language-focused learning: a component of classroom practice in which learners' attention is drawn to particular aspects of language (Nation & Newton, 2009).

languaging: the productive use of language by learners not just to communicate meaning, but actually to solve problems in the second language by trying out different solutions aloud (Swain, 2006).

maturational constraints: the principle that as age increases, so does the difficulty in acquiring native like proficiency in a second language. That is, the ability to gain perfect proficiency in all language domains is limited by biological changes that occur between early childhood and adolescence.

meaning-focused input: an essential component of classroom discourse in which the main purpose of language input for the learner is to communicate information that is comprehensible to the learner (Nation & Newton, 2009).

meaning-focused output: an essential component of classroom discourse in which the main purpose of language production by the learner is to communicate information that is comprehensible to others (Nation & Newton, 2009).

metalinguistic: thinking and talking about language itself using grammatical terminology (for example, 'subject', 'verb', 'adjective') rather than using language to communicate meaning on other topics.

model: (noun, verb) a demonstration of the appropriate and correct use of the language to be acquired; to provide such a demonstration.

motivation: the intensity with which we desire to do something or to attain a goal, how hard we are willing to work at it, and how long we are willing to keep working at it.

native like ability: the ability to understand and use the target language like those who have used the language from a very early age.

negotiation for meaning: (also known as 'negotiated interaction') interaction in which participants employ strategies to overcome or anticipate breakdowns in communication, including modifications to their language and way of talking.

notice: to pay attention to or to register something (for example, a word, a grammatical form, or way of saying something).

noticing hypothesis: the hypothesis of Schmidt (1990, 2001) that learners cannot learn the features of a language that they do not pay attention to, at some level of awareness. In the strong version of this hypothesis, learning requires conscious attention; in the weak version, learning is greater with conscious attention.

NS; NNS ('native speaker'; 'non-native speaker'): now somewhat contentious labels used to distinguish those who have the target language as a first language (NS) or as a second language (NNS). NNS is often now replaced by 'second language user' or 'second language learner'.

off-task: language or behavior that is tangential to the main focus of the task during classroom activity.

output hypothesis: see 'comprehensible output hypothesis'.

paralinguistic: everything we use to communicate beyond words alone, including gesture, facial expressions, pitch, and intonation.

pragmatics: how we communicate in specific contexts with others, including our knowledge of the underlying (nonliteral) meaning of what we say and do—such as the meaning of gestures or phrases— which may mean different things in different contexts, according to where we are, who we are talking to, and about what.

presentational talk: formal language used to display knowledge, including a student 'response' turn in an IRF interaction pattern (Barnes 1976, 2008). In contrast, see 'exploratory talk'.

primary school: (also termed 'elementary school' in North America) the first 6–7 years of formal compulsory schooling (ages 5/6–11/12 years).

procedural knowledge: the ability to use, in meaningful communication, words or rules that may first have been learned explicitly. Procedural knowledge is an essential step toward the development of fluency in oral production. In contrast, see 'declarative knowledge'.

prompts: linguistic and sometimes non-linguistic devices used to support a learner to produce new language or to reformulate what they have produced in a more target like way. In the latter case, it is a form of corrective feedback.

pushed output: the type of language learners produce as they struggle to express themselves and be understood. This involves use of new forms and modification of existing forms (Swain, 1985).

recast: a response to a learner's non-target like utterance that reformulates that utterance into a more target like form, while retaining the same central meaning.

reciprocal, reciprocity: an interactional style that is supportive of the interlocutor, reflected by each participant listening to the other and responding appropriately in a 'give and take' manner.

scaffolded, scaffolding: a joint construction of meaning, in which the participation of one person enables the other to perform a task or produce language that would be too difficult to manage unassisted.

second language: an additional language (whether second, third, fourth, etc.) that is learnt after an individual's first or native language is established. In contrast, see 'foreign language'.

secondary school: following primary school, this is the final four to seven years of formal schooling that in many countries is compulsory (ages 12/13–17/18 years). It differs as to length and administration, with some countries splitting junior and senior schooling.

structured input: spoken or written language that contains particular features; the teacher modifies or presents this language in such a way that leads students to pay attention to these particular language features.

subtractive bilingualism: the effect on one's first language of having less exposure and less use of this language; the increasingly rich exposure to and use of a second language may result in reducing L1 proficiency or even replacing one's first language.

target like: language that is a 'correct' or commonly accepted ('native') form.

ultimate attainment: the long term achievement of language learners.

uptake: the learners' response to linguistic feedback. Uptake may include modification or repair in response to feedback, or simply an acknowledgement of agreement. No uptake is reflected by a lack of response. This term is used more generally to express the use that learners make of feedback.

working memory: a construct of our ability to temporarily store and manipulate pieces of information in memory—vital while communicating, completing a task, or problem solving.

Transcription Conventions

Researchers use a variety of conventions when transcribing oral data. These are preserved in the examples provided in the Classroom Snapshots. Table 6.1 provides a list of those conventions that appear in this book. Sometimes researchers use different conventions for the same purpose; where this occurs, both conventions are listed.

Convention	Example	Meaning
>	**S:** It's a good> it's a good one?	Rising intonation (where a question mark is not used)
XX	**S:** It's on the XX.	Transcriber was unable to decipher the word or part of a word.
[ ]	**S:** This man is more [strong]er than he.	1 Transcriber was unsure what was said, but it sounds like [ ].
	S: [laughs] Your turn. [baby voice, being silly] **S:** Have you a … oh sorry. [locates picture of bread]	2 Transcriber's notes about context, tone of voice, laughter, etc.
	S: *Alle sei.* [At six.]	3 Translation of foreign (non-English) language
:	**S:** That's blu:e. **S:** He is so: big.	Elongated vowel sound
=	**S:** And then he goed to= **T:** =He went? He went to the shop?	Speaker broke off and/or interlocutor interrupted what speaker was saying.
= =	**S:** And then he goed to= **T:** =He went?= He went to the shop?	Spoken over the previous speaker's utterance.
…	**S:** Pasta … is this pasta?	Pause
italics	**S:** *Alle sei.*	Foreign (non-English) language
underline	**S:** No no no I don't know	1 Underlined section is said as a single chunk (formulaic sequence).
	S: *Grattugiano il cioccolato.*	2 Stress on part of a word

Table 6.1 Transcription conventions used in this book

References

Alcón Soler, E. & García Mayo, M. P. (2009). Interaction and language learning in foreign language contexts: Introduction. *International Review of Applied Linguistics, 47*, 239–43.

Alegría, A. & García Mayo, M. P. (2009). Oral interaction in task-based EFL learning: The use of the L1 as a cognitive tool. *International Review of Applied Linguistics, 47*, 325–45.

Anderson, J. (1983). *The architecture of cognition*. Cambridge, MA: Harvard University.

Ando, J., Fukunaga, N., Kurahashi, J., Suto, T., Nakano, T., & Kage, M. (1992). A comparative study on two EFL teaching methods: The communicative and the grammatical approach. *Japanese Journal of Educational Psychology, 40*, 247–56.

Antón, M. & DiCamilla, F. (1998). Socio-cognitive functions of L1 collaborative interaction in the L2 classroom. *Canadian Modern Language Review/La Revue canadienne des langues vivantes, 54*, 314–42.

Au, K. (1980). Participation structures in a reading lesson with Hawaiian children; Analysis of a culturally appropriate instructional event. *Anthropology and Education Quarterly, 11*, 91–115.

August, D. & Shanahan, T. (Eds). (2006). *Developing literacy in second-language learners: Report of the National Literacy Panel on Language-Minority Children and Youth*. Mahwah, NJ: Lawrence Erlbaum Associates.

Baker, N.D. & Nelson, K.E. (1984). Recasting and related conversational techniques for triggering syntactic advances by young children. *First Language, 5*, 3–22.

Barnard, R. (2009). Submerged in the mainstream? A case study of an immigrant learner in a New Zealand primary classroom. *Language and Education, 23*, 233–48.

Barnes, D. (1976). *From communication to curriculum*. Harmondsworth, UK: Penguin.

Barton, D. (1994). *Literacy: An introduction to the ecology of written language*. Oxford: Blackwell.

Batstone R. & Philp, J. (2013). Classroom interaction and learning across time and space. In K. McDonough & A. Mackey (Eds), *Second language interaction in diverse educational contexts* (pp. 109–28). Amsterdam: John Benjamins.

Berk, L. E. (2013). *Child development 9e*. Boston: Pearson Education.

Berman, R. (2007). Language knowledge and use across adolescence. In E. Hoff & M. Shatz (Eds), *Blackwell handbook of language development* (pp. 347–67). Malden, MA: Blackwell.

Birdsong, D. (2005). Interpreting age effects in second language acquisition. In J.Kroll & A. Groot (Eds), *Handbook of Bilingualism: Psycholinguistic Approaches* (pp. 9–49). New York: Oxford University Press.

Blanco-Iglesias, S., Broner, J., & Tarone, E. (1995). Observations of language use in Spanish immersion classroom interactions. In L. Eubank, L. Selinker, W. E. Rutherford, & M. Sharwood Smith (Eds), *The current state of interlanguage: Studies in honor of William E. Rutherford* (pp. 241–54). Amsterdam: John Benjamins.

Britton, J. (1970). *Language and learning*. Harmondsworth, UK: Penguin.

Brooks, F. B., Donato, R., & McGlone, J. V. (1997). When are they going to say "it" right? Understanding learner talk during pair-work activity. *Foreign Language Annals, 30*, 524–41.

Burstall, C. (1975). Factors affecting foreign-language learning: A consideration of some relevant research findings. *Language Teaching and Linguistics Abstracts, 8*, 105–25.

Cazden, C. B. (2001). *Classroom discourse 2e*. Portsmouth, NH: Heinemann Education.

Cekaite, A. (2007). A child's development in interactional competence in a Swedish L2 classroom. *The Modern Language Journal, 91*, 45–62.

Celce-Murcia, M. (1991). Grammar pedagogy in second and foreign language teaching. *TESOL Quarterly, 25*, 459–80.

Celce-Murcia, M. (2001). Language teaching approaches. In Celce-Murcia, M. (Ed.), *Teaching English as a second or foreign language* (pp. 3–11). Boston: Heinle & Heinle.

Chaudron, C. (1988). *Second language classrooms*. Cambridge: Cambridge University Press.

Clay, M. M. (2001). *Change over time in children's literacy development*. Auckland, New Zealand: Heinemann Education.

Corson, D. (2001). *Language diversity and education*. Mawah, NJ: Lawrence Erlbaum Associates.

Coughlan, P. & Duff, P. (1994). Same task, different activities: Analysis of a SLA task from an Activity Theory Perspective. In J. Lantolf & G. Appel (Eds), *Vygotskian perspectives on second language research.* (pp. 173–93). NJ: Ablex.

Cummins, J. (2000). *Language, power, and pedagogy: Bilingual children in the crossfire*. Bristol: Multilingual Matters.

Damon, W. & Phelps, E. (1989). Critical distinctions among three methods of peer education. *International Journal of Educational Research, 13*, 9–20.

DeKeyser, R. (2005). What makes learning second language grammar difficult? A review of issues. *Language Learning, 55*, 1–25.

DeKeyser, R. (2007). *Practice in a second language: Perspectives from applied linguistics and cognitive psychology*. Cambridge: Cambridge University Press.

de la Fuente, M. J. (2002). Negotiation and oral acquisition of L2 vocabulary: The roles of input and output in the receptive and productive acquisition of words. *Studies in Second Language Acquisition, 24*, 81–112.

Dewaele, J. M. & Furnham, A. (1999). Extraversion: The unloved variable in applied linguistic research. *Language Learning, 49*, 509–44.

Dobinson, T. (2001). Do learners learn from classroom interaction and does the teacher have a role to play? *Language Teaching Research, 5*, 189–211.

Dörnyei, Z. (2001a). *Teaching and researching motivation.* London: Longman.

Dörnyei, Z. (2001b). *Motivational strategies in the language classroom.* Cambridge: Cambridge University Press.

Dörnyei, Z. (2005). *The psychology of the language learner: Individual differences in second language acquisition.* Mahwah, NJ: Lawrence Erlbaum Associates.

Dörnyei, Z. (2006). Individual differences in second language acquisition. *AILA Review, 19*, 42–68.

Dörnyei, Z. & Malderez, A. (1997). Group dynamics and foreign language teaching. *System, 25*, 65–81.

Dörnyei, Z. & Murphey, T. (2003). *Group dynamics in the language classroom.* Cambridge: Cambridge University Press.

Doughty, C. & Varela, E. (1998). Communicative focus on form. In C. Doughty & J. Williams (Eds), *Focus on form in classroom second language acquisition* (pp. 114–38). New York: Cambridge University Press.

Duchesne, S., McMaugh, A., Bochner, S., & Krause, K. (2013). *Educational psychology for learning and teaching 4e.* Melbourne: Cengage Learning.

Duff, P. A. (2003). Intertextuality and hybrid discourses: The infusion of pop culture in educational discourse. *Linguistics and Education, 14*, 231–76.

Dunn, J. (1999). Siblings, friends, and the development of social understanding. In W. A. Collins & B. Laursen (Eds), *Relationships as social contexts* (pp. 263–79). Mahwah, NJ: Lawrence Erlbaum.

Early, M. & Marshall, S. (2008). Adolescent ESL students' interpretation and appreciation of literary texts: A case study of multimodality. *Canadian Modern Language Review/La Revue canadienne des langues vivantes, 64*, 377–97.

Edwards, D. & Mercer, N. (1994). Communication and control. In B. Stierer & J. Maybin (Eds), *Language, Literacy and Learning in Educational Practice* (pp. 188–202). Clevedon: Multilingual Matters.

Ellis, R. (2004). Individual differences in second language learning. In A. Davies & C. Elder (Eds), *The handbook of applied linguistics* (pp. 525–51). Oxford: Blackwell.

Ellis, R. (2005). *Instructed second language acquisition: A literature review.* Wellington, New Zealand: New Zealand Ministry of Education. Retrieved from http://www.educationcounts.govt.nz/data/assets/pdf_file/0008/6983/instructed-second-language.pdf

Ellis, R. (2006). Current issues in the teaching of grammar: an SLA perspective. *TESOL Quarterly, 40*, 83–108.

Ellis, R. (2008). Principles of instructed second language acquisition. *CAL Digest, December 2008*, 1–6.

Ellis, R., Basturkmen, H., & Loewen, S. (2001). Learner uptake in communicative ESL lessons. *Language Learning, 51*, 281–318.

Ellis, R., Tanaka, Y., & Yamazaki, A. (1994). Classroom interaction, comprehension, and the acquisition of L2 word meanings. *Language Learning, 44*, 449–91.

Erlam, R. (2003). The effects of deductive and inductive instruction on the acquisition of direct object pronouns in French as a second language. *The Modern Language Journal, 87*, 242–260.

Erlam, R. (2005). Language aptitude and its relationship to instructional effectiveness in second language acquisition. *Language Teaching Research, 9*, 147–71.

Erlam, R. M. & Sakui, K. (2006). *Instructed second language acquisition: Case studies*. Wellington, New Zealand: Ministry of Education.

Ernst-Slavit, G. & Mason, M. R. (2011). Words that hold us up: Teacher talk and academic language in five upper elementary classrooms. *Linguistics and Education, 22*, 430–40.

Ervin-Tripp, S. (1991). Play in language development. In B. Scales, A. Almy, M. Almy, A. Nicolopoulou, & S. M. Ervin-Tripp (Eds), *Play and the social context of development in early care and education* (pp. 84–98). New York: Columbia Teachers College.

Farrar, M. J. (1990). Discourse and the acquisition of grammatical morphemes. *Journal of Child Language, 17*, 607–24.

Fasoli, L. & Johns, V. (2007). Children's services in remote Australian indigenous communities: Practices and challenges. *Canadian Journal of Native Education, 30*, 83–101.

Fassler, R. (1998). Room for talk: Peer support for getting into English in an ESL kindergarten. *Early Childhood Research Quarterly, 13*, 379–409.

Fernald, A. & Simon, T. (1984). Expanded intonation contours in mothers' speech to newborns. *Developmental psychology, 20*, 104–113.

Field, J. (2003). *Psycholinguistics: A resource book for students*. London: Routledge.

Fogle, L. W. (2008). Home-school connections for international adoptees. Repetition in parent-child interaction. In J. Philp, R. Oliver, & A. Mackey (Eds), *Child's play? Second language acquisition and the younger learner* (pp. 280–301). Amsterdam: John Benjamins.

Fountas, I. C. & Pinnell, G. S. (2001). *Guiding readers and writers (grades 3–6): Teaching comprehension, genre, and content literacy*. Portsmouth, NH: Heinemann.

García Mayo, M.P. & Alcon Soler, E. (2002). The role of interaction in instructed language learning. *International Journal of Educational Research, 37*, 3–4.

García Mayo, M.P. (2002). Interaction in advanced EFL pedagogy: a comparison of form-focused activities. *International Journal of Educational Research, 37*, 1–394.

Gass, S. M. (2003). Input and interaction. In C. Doughty & M. Long (Eds), *The Handbook of Second Language Acquisition* (pp. 224–55). Malden, MA: Blackwell.

Gass, S. M. (2013). *Second language acquisition: An introductory course 4e*. New York: Routledge.

Genishi, C. & Dyson, A. H. (1984). *Language assessment in the early years*. Norwood, NJ: Ablex.

Gibbons, P. (1991). *Learning to learn in a second language*. Sydney: Primary English Teaching Association.

Gibbons, P. (2006). *Bridging discourses in the ESL classroom: Students, teachers and researchers*. London: Continuum.

Hakuta, K., Butler, Y. G., & Witt, D. (2000). *How long does it take English learners to attain proficiency?* Santa Barbara, CA: University of California Linguistic Minority Research Institute. Retrieved from http://www.stanford.edu/~hakuta/Publications

Harrington, M. W. & Sawyer, M. (1992). L2 working memory capacity and L2 reading skills. *Studies in Second Language Acquisition, 14, 1*, 25–38.

Hartup, W. W. (1989). Social relationships and their developmental significance. *American Psychologist, 44*, 120–6.

Hartup, W. W. (1992). *Having friends, making friends, and keeping friends: Relationships as educational contexts*. ERIC digest. Urbana, IL: ERIC Clearinghouse on Elementary and Early Childhood Education. Retrieved from the ERIC database. (ED 345854).

Hatch, E. (1983). *Psycholinguistics: a second language perspective*. Rowley, MA: Newbury House.

Hay, I. & Fielding-Barnsley, R. (2009). Competencies that underpin children's transition into early literacy. *Australian Journal of Language and Literacy, 32*, 148–62.

Heath, S. B. (1983). *Ways with words: Language, life and work in communities and classrooms*. Cambridge, MA: Cambridge University Press.

Ho, D. G. E. (2005). Why do teachers ask the questions they ask? *RELC Journal, 36*, 297–310.

Hudelson, S. (1994). Literacy development of second language children. In F. Genesee (Ed.), *Educating second language children: The whole child, the whole curriculum, the whole community* (pp. 129–58). Cambridge: Cambridge University Press.

Hymes, D. H. (1972). On communicative competence. In J. B. Pride & J. Holmes (Eds), *Sociolinguistics: Selected Readings* (pp. 269–93). Harmondsworth: Penguin.

Kormos, J. & Csìzer, K. (2008). Age-related differences in the motivation of learning English as a foreign language: Attitudes, selves and motivated learning behaviour. *Language Learning, 58*, 327–55.

Kowal, M. & Swain, M. (1994). Using collaborative language production tasks to promote students' language awareness. *Language Awareness, 3*, 73–93.

Krashen, S. D. (1985). *The input hypothesis: Issues and implications*. London: Longman.

Kuiken, F. & Vedder, I. (2002). The effect of interaction in acquiring the grammar of a second language. *International Journal of Educational Research, 37*, 343–8.

Lacorte, M. (2005). Teachers' knowledge and experience in the discourse of foreign-language classrooms. *Language Teaching Research, 9(4)*, 381–402.

Lambert, W. (1975). Culture and language as factors in learning and education. In A. Wolfgang (Ed.), *Education in immigrant students* (pp. 55–83). Toronto: Ontario Institute for Studies in Education.

Lantolf, J. P. & Thorne, S. (2006). *Sociocultural theory and the genesis of second language development*. Oxford: Oxford University Press.

Larsen-Freeman, D. (2000). *Techniques and principles in language teaching 2e*. Oxford: Oxford University Press.

Larsen-Freeman, D. & Anderson, M. (2011). *Techniques and principles in language teaching 3e*. Oxford: Oxford University Press.

Lightbown, P. (2013). *Focus on content-based language teaching*. Oxford: Oxford University Press.

Lightbown, P. & Spada, N. (2013). *How languages are learned 4e*. Oxford: Oxford University Press.

Loewen, S. & Philp, J. (2006). Recasts in the adult English L2 classroom: Characteristics, explicitness, and effectiveness. *The Modern Language Journal, 90*, 536–56.

Long, M. H. (1988). Instructed interlanguage development. In L. M. Beebe (Ed.), *Issues in second language acquisition* (pp.115–41). Cambridge, MA: Newbury House.

Long, M. H. (1990). The least a second language acquisition theory needs to explain. *TESOL Quarterly, 24*, 649–66.

Long, M. H. (1996). The role of the linguistic environment in second language acquisition. In W. C. Ritchie & T. K. Bhatica (Eds), *Handbook of research on language acquisition. Second Language Acquisition* (Vol. 2, pp. 413–68). New York: Academic Press.

Long, M. H. (2007). *Problems in SLA*. Mahwah, NJ: Lawrence Erlbaum Associates.

Lyster, R. (1998a). Recasts, repetition, and ambiguity in L2 classroom discourse. *Studies in Second Language Acquisition, 20*, 51–81.

Lyster, R. (1998b). Negotiation of form, recasts, and explicit correction in relation to error type and learner repair in immersion classrooms. *Language Learning, 48*, 183–218.

Lyster, R. (2007). *Learning and teaching language through content: A counterbalanced approach*. Amsterdam: John Benjamins.

Lyster, R. & Mori, H. (2006). Interactional feedback and instructional counterbalance. *Studies in Second Language Acquisition, 28*, 321–41.

Lyster, R. & Ranta, L. (1997). Corrective feedback and learner uptake: Negotiation form in communicative classrooms. *Studies in Second Language Acquisition, 19*, 37–66.

Lyster, R. & Ranta, L. (2013). The case for variety in corrective feedback research. *Studies in Second Language Acquisition, 35*, 167–84.

Lyster, R. & Sato, M. (2013). Skill Acquisition Theory and the role of practice in L2 development. In M. García Mayo, M. Gutierrez Mangado, & M. Martinez Adrian (Eds), *Contemporary approaches to second language acquisition* (pp. 71–92). Amsterdam: John Benjamins.

Mackey, A., Kanganas, A., & Oliver, R. (2007). Task familiarity and interactional feedback in child ESL classrooms. *TESOL Quarterly, 41*, 285–312.

Mackey, A. & Oliver, R. (2002). Interactional feedback and children's L2 development. *System, 30*, 459–77.

Mackey, A., Oliver, R., & Leeman, J. (2003). Interactional input and the incorporation of feedback: An exploration of NS–NNS and NNS–NNS adult and child dyads. *Language Learning, 35*, 35–66.

Mackey, A. & Philp, J. (1998). Conversational interaction and second language development: Recasts, responses, and red herrings? *The Modern Language Journal, 82*, 338–56.

Mackey, A. & Polio, C. (Eds). (2009). *Multiple perspectives on interaction: Second language research in honor of Susan. M. Gass.* New York: Routledge.

Malaguzzi, L. (1996). The right to the environment. In T. Filipini & V. Vecchi (Eds), *The hundred languages of children: The exhibit* (p. 40) Reggio Emilia: Reggio Children.

McKay, P. (2005). Research into the assessment of school-age language learners. *Annual Review of Applied Linguistics, 25*, 243–63.

McLaughlin, B. (1990). Restructuring. *Applied Linguistics, 11*, 113–28.

Mehan, H. (1979). *Learning lessons.* Cambridge, MA: Harvard University Press.

Mercer, N. (1995) *The guided construction of knowledge: talk amongst teachers and learners.* Clevedon: Multilingual Matters.

Mercer, N. & Hodgkinson, S. (Eds). (2008). *Exploring talk in school.* London: Sage Publications.

Miller, J. (2000). Language use, identity and social interaction: Migrant students in Australia. *Research on Language and Social Interaction, 33*, 69–100.

Miller, J. (2003). *Audible difference: ESL and social identity in schools.* Bristol: Multilingual Matters.

Ministry of Education. DVD. (2008). *Making language and learning work 2.* Wellington, New Zealand: Cognition Consulting, Team Solutions and Visual Learning.

Mitchell, R. & Martin, C. (1997). Rote learning, creativity and a 'understanding' in classroom foreign language teaching. *Language Teaching Research, 1*, 1–27.

Miyake, A. & Friedman, N. (1998). Individual differences in second language proficiency: Working memory as language aptitude. In A. Healy & L. E. Bourne (Eds), *Foreign language learning: Psycholinguistic studies on training and retention* (pp. 339–64). Mahwah, NJ: Lawrence Erlbaum Associates.

Mori, J. (2004). Negotiating sequential boundaries and learning opportunities: a case from a Japanese language classroom. *The Modern Language Journal, 88,* 536–50.

Muñoz, C. (2003). Variation in oral skills development and age of onset. In M. P. Garcia Mayo & M. L. Garcia Lecumberri (Eds), *Age and the acquisition of English as a foreign language: Theoretical issues and fieldwork* (pp. 161–81). Bristol: Multilingual Matters.

Muñoz, C. (2006). The effects of age on foreign language learning: The BAF project. In C. Muñoz (Ed.), *Age and the rate of foreign language learning* (pp. 1–40). Bristol: Multilingual Matters.

Muñoz, C. (2007). Age-related differences and second language learning practice. In R. DeKeyser (Ed.), *Practice in a second language. Perspectives from applied linguistics and cognitive psychology* (pp. 229–55). Cambridge, MA: Cambridge University Press.

Muranoi, H. (2007). Output practice in the L2 classroom. In R. M. DeKeyser (Ed.), *Practice in a second language: Perspectives from applied linguistics and cognitive psychology* (pp. 51–84). New York: Cambridge University Press.

Myles, F., Mitchell, R., & Hooper, J. (1999). Interrogative chunks in French L2: A basis for creative construction? *Studies in Second Language Acquisition, 21,* 49–80.

Nation, I. S. P. (2007). The four strands. *Innovation in Language Learning and Teaching, 1,* 2–13.

Nation, I. S. P. (2008). Teaching vocabulary: Strategies and techniques. Boston, MA: Heinle.

Nation, I. S. P. & Laufer, B. (2012). Vocabulary. In S. Gass and A. Mackey (Eds), *The Routledge handbook of second language acquisition* (pp. 136–76). New York: Routledge.

Nation, I. S. P. & Newton, J. (2009). *Teaching ESL/EFL listening and speaking.* London: Taylor & Francis.

O'Donnell, A. M. (2006). The role of peers and group learning. In P. Alexander & P. Winne (Eds), *Handbook of educational psychology 2e* (pp. 781–802). Mahwah, NJ: Lawrence Erlbaum Associates.

Oliver, R. (1995a). Negative feedback in child NS/NNS conversation. *Studies in Second Language Acquisition, 18,* 459–81.

Oliver, R. (1995b). *Negotiation and feedback in child SLA.* (Unpublished doctoral thesis). The University of Western Australia, Crawley, Australia.

Oliver, R. (1997). How different is the input ESL teachers provide to adult and child learners? *TESOL in Context, 7,* 26–30.

Oliver, R. (1998). Negotiation of meaning in child interactions: The relationship between conversational interaction and second language acquisition. *The Modern Language Journal, 82,* 372–86.

Oliver, R. (2000). Age differences in negotiation and feedback in classroom and pair work. *Language Learning, 50,* 119–150.

Oliver, R. (2002). The patterns of negotiation for meaning in child interactions. The *Modern Language Journal, 86,* 97–111.

Oliver, R. (2009a). How young is too young? Investigating negotiation of meaning and corrective feedback in children aged five to seven years. In A. Mackey & C. Polio (Eds), *Multiple perspectives on interaction: Second language research in honor of Susan. M. Gass* (pp. 135–56). New York: Routledge.

Oliver, R. (2009b). Teaching content, learning language: Socialising ESL students into classroom practices. In R. Barnard & M. Torres-Guzman (Eds), *Creating classroom communities of learning: International case studies and perspectives* (pp. 36–52). Bristol: Multilingual Matters.

Oliver, R. & Grote, E. (2010). The provision and uptake of different types of recasts in child and adult ESL learners: What is the role of age and context? *Australian Review of Applied Linguistics 33(3),* 26.1–26.22.

Oliver, R., Haig, Y., & Rochecouste, J. (2004). Adolescent speech networks and communicative competence. *English in Australia, 141,* 49–57.

Oliver, R., Haig, Y., & Rochecouste, J. (2005). Communicative competence in oral language assessment. *Language and Education, 19,* 212–22.

Oliver, R., & Mackey, A. (2003). Interactional context and feedback in child ESL classrooms. *The Modern Language Journal, 87,* 519–533.

Paradis, J. (2007). Second language acquisition in childhood. In E. Hoff & M. Shatz (Eds), *Blackwell handbook of language development* (pp. 387–406). Malden, MA: Blackwell.

Pea, R. (2004). The social and technological dimensions of scaffolding and related theoretical concepts for learning, education and human activity. *The Journal of the Learning Science 13,* 423–51.

Perera, N. (2001). The role of prefabricated language in young children's second

Philp, J. (2003). Constraints on "noticing the gap". *Studies in Second Language Acquisition, 25,* 99–126.

Philp, J., Adams, R., & Iwashita, N. (2013). *Peer interaction and second language learning.* New York: Taylor & Francis.

Philp, J. & Duchesne, S. (2008). When the gate opens: The interaction between social and linguistics goals in child second language development. In J. Philp, R. Oliver, & A. Mackey (Eds), *Child's play? Second language acquisition and the younger learner* (pp. 83–104). Amsterdam: John Benjamins.

Philp, J. & Iwashita, N. (2013). Talking, tuning in, and noticing: Exploring the benefits of output in task based peer interaction, *Language Awareness,* DOI:10.1080/09658416.2012.758128.

Philp, J., Oliver, R., & Mackey, A. (2006). Child's play? Second language acquisition and the younger learner in context: An introduction. In J. Philp, R. Oliver, & A. Mackey (Eds), *Child's play? Second language acquisition and the younger learner* (pp. 3–23). Amsterdam: John Benjamins.

Philp, J. & Tognini, R. (2009). Language acquisition in foreign language contexts and the differential benefits of interaction. *International Review of Applied Linguistics, 47*, 245–66.

Pica, T. (1994). Research on negotiation: What does it reveal about second language learning conditions processes and outcomes? *Language Learning, 44*, 493–527.

Pica, T. (2013). From input, output and comprehension to negotiation, evidence, and attention. In M. García Mayo, M. Gutierrez Mangado, & M. Martinez Adrian (Eds), *Contemporary approaches to second language acquisition* (pp. 49–70). Amsterdam: John Benjamins.

Pienemann, M. & Johnston, M. (1987). Factors influencing the development of language proficiency. In D. Nunan (Ed.), *Applying second language acquisition research* (pp. 45–141). Adelaide: National Curriculum Resource Centre, AMEP.

Platt, E. & Brooks, F. B. (1994). The "acquisition-rich environment" revisited. *The Modern Language Journal, 78*, 497–511.

Ranta, L. (2002). The role of learners' language analytic ability in the communicative classroom. In P. Robinson (Ed.), *Individual differences and instructed language learning* (pp. 159–79). Amsterdam: John Benjamins.

Richards, J. C. & Rodgers, T. S. (2001). *Approaches and methods in language teaching 2e*. Cambridge: Cambridge University Press.

Robinson, P. (2005). Aptitude and second language acquisition. *Annual Review of Applied Linguistics, 25*, 46–73.

Sachs, J., Bard, B., & Johnson, M. (1981). Language learning with restricted input: Case studies of two hearing children of deaf parents. *Applied Psycholinguistics, 2*, 33–54.

Sáfár, A. & Kormos, J. (2008). Revisiting problems with foreign language aptitude. *International Review of Applied Linguistics in Language Teaching, 46*, 113–36.

Saxton, M. (1997). The contrast theory of negative input. *Journal of Child Language, 24*, 139-161.

Scarcella, R. C. & Higa, C. (1981). Input, negotiation, and age difference in second language acquisition. *Language Learning, 31*, 409–32.

Schmidt, R. (1990). The role of consciousness in second language learning. *Applied Linguistics, 11*, 129–58.

Schmidt, R. (2001). Attention. In P. Robinson (Ed.), *Cognition and second language instruction* (pp. 3–32). Cambridge: Cambridge University Press.

Segalowitz, N. (2003). Automaticity and second language acquisition. In C. Doughty & M. Long (Eds), *The handbook of second language acquisition* (pp. 382–408). Oxford: Blackwell Publishers.

Shahraki, S. H. & Kassaian, Z. (2011). Effects of learner interaction, receptive and productive learning tasks on vocabulary acquisition: An Iranian case. *Procedia-Social and Behavioral Sciences, 15*, 2165–2171.

Sheen, Y. (2006). Exploring the relationship between characteristics of recasts and learner uptake. *Language Teaching Research, 10*, 361–92.

Skehan, P. (1986). The role of foreign language aptitude in a model for school learning. *Language Testing, 3*, 188–221.

Skehan, P. (1998). *A cognitive approach to language learning*. Oxford: Oxford University Press.

Snow, C., Griffin, P., & Burns, M. S. (Eds). (2005). *Knowledge to support the teaching of reading: Preparing teachers for a changing world*. San Francisco: Jossey-Bass.

Snow, C. E. & Hoefnagel-Höhle, M. (1978). The critical period for language acquisition: Evidence from second language learning. *Child Development, 49*, 1114–1128.

Spada, N. (2007). Communicative language teaching. *International handbook of English language teaching, 15*, 271–88.

Spada, N. & Lightbown, P. (2008). Form-focused instruction: Isolated or integrated? *TESOL Quarterly, 42*, 181–207.

Strong, M. (1983). Social styles and the second language acquisition of Spanish-speaking kindergartners. *TESOL Quarterly, 17*, 241–58.

Swain, M. (1985). Communicative competence: Some roles of comprehensible input and comprehensible output in its development. In S. Gass & C. Madden (Eds), *Input in second language acquisition* (pp. 235–53). Rowley, MA: Newbury House.

Swain, M. (1993). The output hypothesis: Just speaking and writing aren't enough. *Canadian Modern Language Review/La Revue canadienne des langues vivantes, 50*, 158–64.

Swain, M. (1995). Three functions of output in second language learning. In G. Cook & B. Seidlhofer (Eds), *For H.G. Widdowson: Principles and practice in the study of language: A festschrift on the occasion of his 60th birthday* (pp. 125–44). Oxford: Oxford University Press.

Swain, M. (2000). The output hypothesis and beyond: Mediating acquisition through collaborative dialogue. In J. P. Lantolf (Ed.), *Sociocultural theory and second language learning* (pp. 97–114). Oxford: Oxford University Press.

Swain, M. (2005). The output hypothesis: Theory and research. In E. Hinkel (Ed.), *The handbook of research in second language teaching and learning* (pp. 471–83). Mahwah, NJ: Lawrence Erlbaum Associates.

Swain, M. (2010). Talking-it-through: Languaging as a source of learning. In R. Batstone (Ed.), *Sociocognitive perspectives on language use and language learning* (pp. 112–30). Oxford: Oxford University Press.

Swain, M. & Lapkin, S. (1998). Interaction and second language learning: Two adolescent French immersion students working together. *The Modern Language Journal, 82*, 320–37.

Swain, M. & Lapkin, S. (2000). Task-based second language learning: The uses of the first language. *Language Teaching Research, 4*, 251–74.

Swain, M. & Lapkin, S. (2001). Focus on form through collaborative dialogue: Exploring task effects. In M. Bygate, P. Skehan, & M. Swain (Eds), *Researching pedagogic tasks: Second language learning, teaching and testing* (pp. 99–118). London: Longman.

Tabors, P. O. & Snow, C. E. (1994). English as a second language in preschool programs. In F. Genesee (Ed.), *Educating second language children: The whole child, the whole curriculum, the whole community* (pp. 103–25). Cambridge: Cambridge University Press.

Tarone, E. & Liu, G. (1995). Situational context, variation and SLA theory. In G. Cook & B. Seidlhofer (Eds), *Principle and practice in applied linguistics: Studies in honour of H. G. Widdowson* (pp. 107–24). Oxford: Oxford University Press.

Tarone, E. & Swain, M. (1995). A sociolinguistic perspective on second language use in immersion classrooms. *The Modern Language Journal, 79*, 166–78.

Tognini, R. (2008). *Interaction in languages other than English classes in Western Australian primary and secondary schools: Theory, practice and perceptions.* (Unpublished doctoral thesis). Edith Cowan University, Australia.

Tognini, R. & Oliver, R. (2012). L1 use in primary and secondary foreign language classrooms and its contribution to learning. In E. Alcon & M. P. Safont (Eds), *Language learners' discourse in instructional settings* (pp. 53–78). Amersterdam: Rodopi.

Tognini, R., Philp, J., & Oliver, R. (2010). Rehearsing, conversing, working it out: second language use in peer interaction. *Australian Review of Applied Linguistics, 33*, 28.1–28.25.

Toohey, K. (1998). "Breaking them up; taking them away": ESL students in grade one. *TESOL Quarterly, 32*, 61–84.

Toohey, K. (2000). *Learning English at school: Identity, social relations, and classroom practice.* Clevedon: Multilingual Matters.

Toohey, K. & Day, E. (1999). Language-learning: The importance of access to community. *TESL Canada Journal, 17*, 40–53.

Topping, K. & Ehly, S. (1998). Introduction to peer-assisted learning. In K. Topping & S. Ehly (Eds), *Peer-assisted learning* (pp. 1–24). Mahwah, NJ: Lawrence Erlbaum Associates.

Toth, P. D., Wagner, E., & Moranski, K. (2013). 'Co-constructing' explicit L2 knowledge with high school Spanish learners through guided induction. *Applied Linguistics, 34*(3), 279–303.

Van Patten, B. & Wiliams, J. (2007). *Theories of second language acquisition.* Mahwah, NJ: Lawrence Erlbaum Associates.

Verhoeven, L. & Vermeer, A. (2002). Communicative competence and personality dimensions in first and second language learners. *Applied Psycholinguistics, 23*, 361–74.

Vygotsky, L. S. (1978). *Mind in society: The development of higher psychological processes*. Cambridge, MA: Harvard University Press.

Westgate, D., J. Batey, Brownlee, J., & Butler, M. (1985). Some characteristics of interaction in foreign language classrooms, *British Educational Research Journal 11*, 271–81.

White, J. (2008). Speeding up acquisition of his and her: Explicit L1/L2 contrasts help. In J. Philp, R. Oliver, & A. Mackey (Eds), *Second language acquisition and the younger learner* (pp. 191–230). Amsterdam: John Benjamins.

White, J., Muñoz, C., & Collins, L. (2007). The his/her challenge: Making progress in a 'regular' L2 programme. *Language Awareness, 16*, 278–99.

White, J. & Ranta, L. (2002). Examining the Interface between Metalinguistic Task Performance and Oral Production in a Second Language, *Language Awareness, 11*, 259–90.

White, L. (1987). Against comprehensible input: the input hypothesis and the development of second language competence. *Applied Linguistics, 8*, 95–110.

Willett, J. (1995). Becoming first graders in an L2: An ethnographic study of L2 socialization. *TESOL Quarterly, 29*, 473–503.

Williams, M. & Burden, R. L. (1997). *Psychology for language teachers*. Cambridge: Cambridge University Press.

Wong Fillmore, L. (1976). *The second time around: Cognitive and social strategies in second language acquisition*. (Unpublished doctoral dissertation). Standford University, Stanford.

Wong Fillmore, L. (1979). Individual differences in second language acquisition. In C. Fillmore, D. Kempler & W. S.-Y. Wang (Eds), *Individual differences in language ability and language behavior* (pp. 203–28). New York: Academic Press.

Wong Fillmore, L. (1985). When Does Teacher Talk Work as Input? In S. Gass & C. Madden, (Eds), *Input in second language acquisition*. (pp. 17–50). Rowley, MA: Newbury House.

Wong Fillmore, L. & Snow, C. (2000). *What teachers need to know about language*. Washington, DC: ERIC Clearinghouse on Language and Linguistics. Retrieved from the ERIC database. ED 990008.

Wood, D., Bruner, J. S., & Ross, G. (1976). The role of tutoring in problem solving. *Journal of Child Psychology and Psychiatry, 17*, 89–100.

Wray, A. (2002). *Formulaic language and the lexicon*. Cambridge: Cambridge University Press.

Index

Page numbers annotated with 'g' or 't' refer to glossary entries or tables respectively.